ZIMBOLICIOUS ANTHOLOGY:

An Anthology of Zimbabwean Literature and Arts,

VOLUME 4

Edited by Tendai R. Mwanaka
Jabulani Mzinyathi

Cover art: Eyes of Truth- of ever-including circles © Tendai R Mwanaka

Mwanaka Media and Publishing Pvt Ltd,
Chitungwiza Zimbabwe
*
Creativity, Wisdom and Beauty

Publisher: Mmap
Mwanaka Media and Publishing Pvt Ltd
24 Svosve Road, Zengeza 1
Chitungwiza Zimbabwe
mwanaka@yahoo.com
www.africanbookscollective.com/publishers/mwanaka-media-and-publishing
https://facebook.com/MwanakaMediaAndPublishing/

Distributed in and outside N. America by African Books Collective
orders@africanbookscollective.com
www.africanbookscollective.com

ISBN: 978-1-77906-504-9
EAN: 9781779065049

©Tendai Rinos Mwanaka 2019

DISCLAIMER
All views expressed in this publication are those of the author and do not necessarily reflect
the views of *Mmap*.

Table of Contents

About editors

Tendai Rinos Mwanaka is a publisher, editor, mentor, thinker, literary artist, visual artist and musical artist with over 30 books published. He writes in English and Shona. His work has appeared in over 400 journals and anthologies from over 27 countries, translated into Spanish, Bengali, Tamil, Russian, Albanian, Macedonian, Serbian, Arabic, French and German

Jabulani Mzinyathi is a free verse, stream of consciousness poet. Driven by righteous indignation he has no sacred cows. *Under The Steel Yoke*, his solo collection is a product of righteous indignation. Next in line in a collection entitled *Righteous Indignation*. Jabulani is a Gweru born poet who is an ex teacher, ex magistrate and is currently a lawyer in private practice.

Contributors's Bio Notes

Tanaka Chidora is a lecturer at the University of Zimbabwe where he teaches Theories of Literature; Popular Culture and Literature; and Creative Writing. He is working on two novels, *Magamba Hostels: a memoir that is not a memoir*, and *Zupco Diaries*. He is also a poet who posts his stuff on many social media platforms. Recently, he submitted a collection of these poems titled *Because Sadness is Beautiful?* for publication.

Matthew K. Chikono is a young speculative fiction writer from the streets of Chitungwiza. He has written numerous short stories and comic books over the years, expressing deep rooted ideas of an ideal African societal, economical and political set up. His pen is currently crafting a speculative novella, titled *Invisible Trails* which is due for the public eye before year's end.

Troy Da Costa says, "It is with feelings of humble fortitude and privilege I once again get to contribute to this worthy project. I hope it inspires poets of all ages to engage in the mathematics of language to create beautiful work to showcase the vast and enigmatic culture of Zimbabweans. If anything is to be learnt from the events of the past year it is we as a nation can no longer walk head low and silent, we are brightly coloured flowers and we deserve to shine. Writers and poets of skill and passion can mirror our society and effect change by showing its ills and illuminating its strengths. This is your task and your duty and the reason art and literature exist.

Andrew Huje is a poet, short story writer and graphic artist who has his works published in *Writers Space Africa* magazine, *Deems* which was published by Deems Literature, *Zimbolicious Volume 3*, and also has published his works in *Brainsores*, a collection of poetry.

Prosper Kavunika is a social commentator whose expresses himself through poetry and short stories. Born in the dormitory town of Chitungwiza, he did both his primary and high school in the same town. Much of his work has been published in online magazines such as *Tuck magazine, poetry corner* and various journals published through *Miombo publishing*.

Nicole Vimbai Kazembe is a twenty-four year old female avid although inexpert poetry writer on a mission to become a professional one, with a poetry book being edited for publishing. When not writing, she enjoys reading and procrastinating while watching television and she is working on a short story book.

Christopher 'Voice' Kudyahakudadirwe is a Zimbabwean freelance writer, photographer, poet and teacher living and working in South Africa. He recently published a collection of short stories entitled *The Big Noise and Other Noises*. His poems have been published in an anthology entitled *Harvest: The University of the Western Cape Masters in Creative Writing Poetry Anthology 2016* and on his poetry blog: https://kudyahakudadirwe.wordpress.com/. He holds a Masters in Creative Writing from the University of the Western Cape. He is currently in the process of enrolling for a PhD in Creative Writing.

Ruvimbo Mafukidze (Poetrue) being a charismatic feminist and business oriented leader with the calabash of poetic healing who has penned a number of poems not published is a Sagittarius, born and bred in the city of Chitungwiza. She did her Primary and Secondary education and commenced her studies in Human Resources Management in 2018.

Trust Mauyasva A B.A Honours in English Literature graduate from the University of Zimbabwe who is passionate about words. He is a writer, poet and blogger who is determined to improve the status of art in society and assist in the promotion of often marginalised art and artists.

Mandhla A Mavolwane is a poet and a spoken word artist who writes and performs to entertain, educate and enlighten the masses on the issues affecting our past, present and future. He is currently studying for an undergraduate honours degree in Psychology at the Midlands State University. In terms of his artistry, his poems have been published in *Best New African Poets 2016, 2017 and 2018 anthologies, Africa, UK and Ireland: Writing Politics and Knowledge Production Volume 1* and *Zimbolicious Volume 3*. Recently he published his first anthology called *Ghetto Symphony* which can be found on this link
http://www.africanbookscollective.com/books/ghetto-symphony

Osman Shato Mbindi (Shato the poet) is a Zimbabwean writer. He is passionate in painting African images; safeguard its identity and pride. He has published a single anthology entitled, "Life and the other side of it", and contributed on poetry international, standard newspaper and on "Pain or Pleasure" by Mc Kenias (2019).

Tinashe Muchuri is a blogger, award winning journalist, performer, poet, storyteller and writer based in Harare. His poetry appears in several online and print magazines, Shona and English anthologies including *Zimbolicious Poetry Anthology Volume 1*. He is the writer of *Zvipfuyo Nevana Vazvo* and *Chibarabada*.

Benniah Munengwa is a poet and reviewer for one of the major Zimbabwean newspapers, *The Daily News*

Victor Gordon Musara is a poet from Ngundu currently working on his debut novel. He's an active contributor for poetrybits.com magazine and the online platforms hellopoetry.com and Mirakee.

Nicholas Mwanaka is part of the first generation of Zimbabwean Shona Language poets, with several poems in various Shona Poetry anthologies that have been used in Zimbabwe's School Curriculums over the years. He has published two plays and a novel and is currently working on another novel

My name is **Tapuwa Mwedzi** born in 1980 on the 1st of January. I was raised by a single parent which partly inspires some of the poems. After a long struggle pursuing tertiary education I graduated in 2017 and am working as a social worker in South Africa.

Philani A. Nyoni is a storyteller, poet, filmmaker and actor based in Bulawayo, Zimbabwe

Clesirdia Nzorozwa is a female poet, hip hop artist, song, short story and script writer aged 21. Her Nationality is Zimbabwean, She has poems that have been published in the Zimbabwean New Standard News Paper several times. Poems such as The Slums, Primrose, Don't you forget etc. Egypt and Afrika are two of her pieces which also featured in the 'Don't Give Up Africa' anthology by different poets from *VaChikepe and the 100 sailors* which is available on Amazon. She also appears on ZTV spoken word programme reciting her pieces titled *Afrika, Jingle bells* etc.

Nicky Rosselli is a landscape artist, but she is also well known for her ink and charcoal drawings of animals. Born and raised on a farm in

Zimbabwe she spent a lot of time exploring the veldt as a child and her love of the African landscape has developed from this. Her interest lies in capturing the dynamics of the landscape and exploring the relationship of figures and animals in the environment. She studied Fine Art at the University of Natal and subsequently worked as a graphic artist in the advertising industry before becoming a secondary school art teacher. She ran the Rosselli Gallery in Masvingo, Zimbabwe, for 10 years. Visit Nicky's website: http://www.rosselli.co.za

Sally Scott is an award winning South African fibre and landscape artist, whose work has been widely exhibited throughout South Africa and internationally. She was born and raised in Zimbabwe, spent 10 years in Botswana, before moving to South Africa in 2000 and now runs a private art studio in Grahamstown, Eastern Cape. Known for her versatility and innovation, Sally's work is imbued with an authentic African spirit. She has a deep commitment to Africa, to the landscape, its flora, fauna and its people. She is passionate about Nature; disturbed by the careless disregard with which it is treated and concerned about the loss of wilderness, which she believes plays a vital role in keeping the balance and maintaining a healthy, functioning world. Website: www.sallyscott.co.za

Kabelo Sithole is an aspiring poet from Bulawayo and is currently a student at Midlands State University. Born in 1997, early encounters with poetry were through rap, but after studying O level literature admiration turned to love when he found that poetry makes him happy.

Zimbabwe-born **Anthony Stidolph (Aka Stidy)** is an award-winning political cartoonist, as well as a painter, writer, columnist and book reviewer who operates from his studio in the beautiful Karkloof Valley in the KwaZulu-Natal Midlands of South Africa. He is also a keen birder and inveterate traveller. Anthony has a blog: https://stidyseye.home.blog/

Michael White: I was born on 18th of June 1997. Fascinated by the art of writing and literature which I believe are products of introspection. Writing poems is my way to subside my emotions during dog days and the way I communicate deep seated my feelings. All forms of art are inherent gifts, I found mine.

Pardon Sikula Moyo was born on the fifteenth of June nineteen ninety five (1995). He was born and raised in Lower Gweru Rural Residential Area in Zimbabwe. He is a second born in a family of five. He did his primary and secondary education at Maboleni primary and secondary schools. He then proceeded to the University of Zimbabwe where he is currently doing his second-year degree program in Social Work this year 2019.

Sheila Banda was born in Zvishavane and is a Librarian in Bulawayo. Passionate about writing, loves Chimamanda Ngozie Adichie's and Tsitsi Dangarembga's works. Believes in woman empowerment and that unity and hope achieves the unimaginable. Her first set of poetry was published in *Zimbolicious Poetry Anthology Volume 3*.

INTRODUCTION

Welcome to the latest addition of the Zimbolicious family: *Zimbolicious Anthology: An Anthology of Zimbabwean Literature and Arts, Volume 4*. The mid-wives have done their bit and a fourth Zimbolicious child has come into the world. It is time to celebrate.

The latest Zimbolicious offering has nonfiction writing, the usual dosage of poetry, an interview, fiction and incisive visual art. Coming up with volume four was not an easy task at all. Works were received from regular contributors, but it was also pleasing to note that the Zimbolicious stable has been joined by relatively new artists.

Zimbolicious Volume Four features poems in the English language; ChiShona poems with translations into the English language are also featured. These works tackle a variety of themes. The poets with their collective audacious eye keenly observe society and reveal the pimples, warts and all that is afflicting the society; talk about the dying, already dead and decaying Zimbabwean currency or nonexistent currency, the emancipation of women, the grinding poverty and the political challenges Zimbabwe faces, others deal with spirituality and religion, love, growing up without a father figure etc…

Nonfiction work leaves one under a barrage of questions. What it means to be a Zimbabwean is put under serious scrutiny. The concept of home is well dissected by a razor sharp scalpel like a surgeon's knife. There is in-depth use of texts written about Zimbabwe, and texts that are being written on Zimbabwe now as the writers argue, interpose, imbues, and disagree with each other, and sometimes agree on what is wrong with being a Zimbabwean, about our identity, about our humanness, and our sense of belonging and home. There is also a concerted focus on defining and dissecting Zimbabwe's literature, writing, self-publishing, and the difficult authorship in an almost impossible economic and political environment that Zimbabwe has been for over two decades.

That adage that a picture tells more than a thousand words is evident in the visual art section of this Zimbolicious. Some delicious slices of scenic Zimbabwean landscape is featured, and images that show people doing various activities are also featured. And like the nonfiction, there is a continuation in investigating what home is in these visual art pieces

The fiction is speculative, bittersweet and stays on your mind like a memory of that long, long forgotten summer of love as each fictionist dealt with issues to do with relationships, love, the lack of, the impermanence of which is an ever recurring leitmotiv in these works, thus therefore, Zimbolicious Volume Four is a must read, robust, incisive collection of Zimbabwean Literature and the arts.

Screw the Zimbabwean!
Tendai R. Mwanaka

From far off memory the story of Zimbabwe or Zimbabweans has been of screwing and being screwed. We love being screwed. We screw each other. If you like screwing please go to Zimbabwe. Here, it's a Zimbabwe of both black and white. The Shona people screwed the Khoi people off their land, then the Shona were screwed by the Ndebele, the Ndebele and Shona were screwed by the Whites, and these as returned favour, screwed the Whites. Blacks screwed Whites, Whites screwed Blacks, throw in the Indians, Chinese, Coloureds etc …it's a *screwing screw, screw screw zhiiim zhiim pot*. It's the sounds of the screws and drill machine, filling every hole it is holeing into. Mugabe screwed the Zimbabweans for over 37 years, and we allowed him to screw us as we moaned with pleasure. *Ummm, aaaah, ishsss….,* Please note Zimbabweans love being screwed so don't mistake the noise they make when they are being screwed by their politicians as pain. No, it's pleasure!

When Mugabe was done screwing the Zimbos, he left it to his protégé to continue screwing them. Hear them now as they moan! *"There is no food", "There is no fuel", "There is no electricity", "There is no water", "There is no foreign currency", "There is not enough school fees", "There is no transport", "There are no jobs", "There is no industry", "There is no president", "There is no hope", "There is no this", "There is no that and those ones"* Even you can hear the mournful sounds in these noises. They are actually enjoying being screwed. They allowed for that.

When you think you know so much, and the Zimbabweans boast about being the most educated people in Africa- I am sure you have heard of this noise- in actual fact you don't know a thing. You should be learning. You should be growing. You should be adapting.

Tell me why would a people who hated what Robert did to them for 37 years, would allow the same screwer to get away with all that he stole, all the sadness and pain he visited upon them. They all agreed to leave Robert alone and let him rest. I am sure the old screwer still chuckles at the Zimbabweans with unbelief at how he got away with all that! If he was that bad he should be rotting in jail. Screw human dignity, where is the human dignity for the millions he screwed for a lifetime, screw mercies and the we-are-the-most-civilized-people-on-the-continent self-hypnosis, screw the Zimbabweans and their civilized poverty of mind and existence!

This would have served as a reminder to Mnangagwa that if he screws us he will eventually face the same screws, but no, we didn't. Now Mnangagwa is happily screwing us left, right and centre and we are enjoying it. Sideways, backwards, in the mouth, every hole is filled up as the crocodile drills us. And mark my words, the next in line will come and screw us. You can go and debate who you think is the next in line but for sure he will screw us, whether it's the, *it will work*, soldier... Note: yes it will work in screwing us, or whether it's the little boycrazywarhead power gloat, screwbag of opposition politics. He so loves moaning about how Mnangagwa is screwing us whilst he is screwing us himself.

So to you African brother and sister out there when you see a Zimbabwean, know that he is screwier screwable. Try to screw him. South Africa, I didn't say do xenophobia on him, just screw him. You are asking me how? It's very simple, just screw his malleable mind. And he will never let go of you! You American, Russian, Indian, Chinese, European, Asian... come to the African tropical paradise of screwing and enjoy yourself. And I tell you, the Zimbabwean will be so grateful for the screwing!

The philosophies of negativity of home as captured by poetry in the 21st Century

Tinashe Muchuri

What is home? Where is home? Is home a geographical space on earth or a perspective taking into consideration of pan-Africanism where Africans take the whole continent as a home for everyone? Where is home considering the call for one people one world through globalisation? Different scholars give home differing definitions. Brian Chikwava in his debut novel 'Harare North' refer to home as just a state of mind. The compilers of The Power of Ideas section in McDougal Littel Literature describes home as not the house one lives in but a place wherever one feels most comfortable and secure.

Reading through Batsirai Chigama's title poem to her debut poetry collection, *gather the children* in which she ask Africa and individual countries in the continent to gather children back home from the raging fires of South Africa, my anxiety of what home is was intrigued and was soon send on a long tour of poetry by Chigama's peers during the period her *gather the children* is interrogating.

Instead of finding an answer the poets send me through conversations and dialogues they had in different anthologies and collections which revolve around the question what is home and where is home? Is the home in 21st century still the same as that of the 19th century and beyond?

Most of the voices in poems published in the era that inspires Chigama and her peers were worried of a home that was disintegrating and falling apart, where children were no longer interested and proud to live and cherish home yet others felt it is good for home to be left and sometimes visit those still feel the place habitable.

According to the voice in Edmond Shonhiwa's poem, *'The Inferno echoes'* which speaks to the xenophobic attacks of migrant workers by South Africans in the year 2008, Africa is home to every son and daughter of the continent but surprisingly other brothers and sisters were at the throat of their kith and kin. The voice asks why?

> *"This Africa is our mamaland*
> *But you cast my children into the inferno*
> *Where they diminish into ashes*
> *Why, brother Azania, Why?"*

Azania is the name that the liberation parties were proposing to rename South Africa after attaining majority rule from apartheid which never was to be. The voice asks has the brother forgotten that this home is for everyone.

A voice in Audrey Lindani Mutinhiri's poem *'Can we have One Africa?'* concur that indeed Africa is home for every African as it reminds the world and everyone with the ears to hear that;

> *"We are one*
> *We are all Africa's children*
> *We cannot suffer injustice,*
> *From both oppressors and our brothers!"*

Instead of the brothers in South Africa to love their brother they played the role of Cain of the Holly Bible who killed his brother, accusing him of receiving honour before God. The South Africans seem to have forgotten that theirs is not a home for them alone but a home for all Africans. Therefore setting their kith and kin on fire was not a good act. With the historical accounts of Bantu migration where people are said to have moved from the area of the Great Lakes stretching down to the South where they moved again northwards running away from Tshaka Zulu during the Nguni incursion, this assertion seem to confirm the history.

But this torture and denial by brothers and people around the world doesn't stop the voice in Noreen Sadziwa's poem, *"My Dream Home"* which speaks to the plight of woman regarded barren and childless in a country where people believe a young sister's children are the elder sister's children. Where has our Ubuntu/unhu/vumunhu/vunhu gone to? Home is here symbolised as the barren mother whose children run away from. Children of Africa are scattered all over the world because mother is not gathering enough food to sustain her children's lives. The same children even as they

4

grow into adults fails to stand by mother as they run to other homes where children of those mothers are helping shape the beauty of their mothers and women. And Africa is surviving on imports and heavily indebted because of borrowing and borrowing.

The voice hears the woman crying;

> *"A woman wails*
> *It's the order of the day*
> *Abused because she is barren."*

The barren woman knows no peace, bile is poured on her wounds, being reopened everyday by venom filled words thrown at her by the people foreign and local. But this is not the home that the voice in the poem dreams of? This home of wailing women is not home. How can it be home when there is wailing voices that indicates to misunderstanding, toiling, warring, discomfort, and despair reigned by fear?

The voice in Mutinhiri's poem *'Family I Have None'* is mourning the absence of home because she is also barren and accused of causing her own plight. If home is home because of the presence of women in it, women alone without men also wail as there are other things, chores, jobs that are done by men only for the home to be inhabitable. This is a voice of homelessness person living as a squatter in a home that is said to be for everyone yet this voice lives in squalid conditions.

> *"I have wandered and slept in the streets*
> *Under cardboard boxes and plastics*
> *I have been the recipient on the litter*
> *I have been called names,*
> *'Mzawangendaba'.*

Where one comes from, or the land of migrant workers' birth is always under fire for neglecting their children, surrendering the best labour and brains to menial jobs in foreign lands where some come back with no glittering riches that attracted them to, in some instances, illegally cross the border, is what the voice in Lilian Dube's poem 'He is Back': which illustrate that the greener pastures attracting children to foreign lands is not all that green as seen from afar.

> *"He left home*
> *And two unborn sons*
> *Five years ago*
> *Skipped the border*
> *Landed in Yeoville*
> *Or was it Hillbrow?"*

The narrator of the story is not even aware of the facts because the man who has just returned has not been in contact with home. Many people have gone and disappeared and they never communicated with people back in the villages and sometimes were assumed dead, or consumed by the vast waters of Limpopo River. The voice continues to describe the state that the person has come back home in. Home to some people is the place to which they get buried. This is the place they will lay forever, which others call the rest place while another group of people call it a place of birth and others say it is a place where one is sheltered.

And the voice in Dube's poem ends with;

> *"He came back*
> *Three days ago-*
> *There is he*
> *There, face up*
> *In the roughhewn*
> *Coffin that has just*
> *Bankrupted his mother –"*

Here we can see a dialogue of voices thinking and asking the same questions, interrogating the era and painting agonies of the time with colours of pain. The voice in Mgcini Nyoni's poem, *'Ten years across the Limpopo'* is a dialogue as they seem sitting at a bridge sharing intoxicating Bronko, the Bronclear cough Syrup in Dube's poem, as it affirms the same plight of people who went to the diaspora and come back to their place of birth with nothing on them except sickness and a hope for a decent burial, costing those who were left behind. These are the people who regard home as a burial place they come to only when death beckons.

> *"What he brought back home is this:*
> *A fruit knife*
> *Known as okapi*
> *The clothes on his back*
> *A small radio*
> *And the deadly*
> *disease that's doggedly*
> *eating him."*

The voice in Charles Mungoshi's *'The Man Who Ran Away From Pain'* paints a picture of those people who ran away from home, whose eyes have been opened and now they have realised how pain is universal. Always get the unexpected results. Some find the going tougher than from the situation they ran away from.

> *"He ran away from home*
> *Where, he thought, all pain*
> *Began.*
> *He went to another country*
> *Where he discovered*
> *The pain of leaving home."*

Can this be said of those hiding away from the authorities of the countries of their economic refuge fearing being deported back with nothing on them or those holding onto asylum, gotten through the lying tooth? The voice here points to home as the place of birth.

Maybe this is the reason why the voice in Tinashe Mushakavanhu's poem 'Tomorrow is long coming' is lamenting of the pain of leaving home, where it says;

> *"Homesickness is a bird that sings to dawn*
> *While it's dark. Is the tree outside a forest*
> *To itself? Or time frozen in obeisance?"*

And another voice in Mushakavanhu's poem 'In the House of Exile' stays in fear as the town that the voice ran to is not embracing. Only the forest or the trees are embracing as they don't chose to whom among the citizens and residents will inhale their oxygen. Could this be the genesis of xenophobic attack? Why is the world not home for every human being?

> *"This town I have adopted*
> *Snoops at me suspiciously*
> *Veiled in the colour of its skin*
> *Blind to my dark present*
> *Only the green breathes*
> *Clean air."*

Here is where the voice in Chigama's 'gather the children' instructs mother to gather her children. The voice is not concerned about those said to be prodigal sons and daughters but the ones mother let go after failing to feed them.

> *"I mean the ones you exiled, choked with despair*
> *Drove across borders with sjamboks of hunger*
> *Now they gingerly carry the stipes*
> *Even as death surrounds them."*

One would ask though whether mother is that selective of her children. Does mother select to dine with the good or embrace all her children hoping they will change for the better? If the home becomes selective, is it home then?

As for the voice in Ignatius Mabasa's poem 'Anxious Land' the 'land has fallen and there is no place to call home', as it accuses some fool who have decided to hang Zimbabwe which most people were calling home. The voice further alleges that the fool hung Zimbabwe's dirty without washing her linen or even bathing her body. Besides the home that is physical, the voice also talks about a spiritual home promised to congregants by the Word of God through the coming of Jesus Christ.

> *"If we don't slump, like fallen baobab,*
> *We will never fall again*
> *Until Christ's Kingdom comes.*
> *For when He comes*
> *There shall not be left one stone upon another,*
> *That shall not be thrown down."*

This voice speaks of a spiritual home promised with the coming of Jesus Christ.

Or is home the nest called by a voice in David Mungoshi's poem 'The Empty Nest' in which new lessons has been learnt, that human beings are like birds and that they own nests which they sometimes should fly away from to rest from the routine. Is it routine of foodlessness home, unemployment or idleness, or just a desire to chart own destinies?

> *"Over the years I have learned my lessons very well*
> *Lesson one: everyone is a bird and has a nest*
> *Lesson two: most birds fly and so must we*
> *Lesson three: we all go away some time to rest*
> *From the routine"*

A nest is a place of birth, of every bird thus making home also a place of birth for people. Africa is home no matter where one is born at in the continent, where we only fly out of to reach our destinies and, come back after touring other places as residents or mere workers.

The voice in Lazarus Sauti's poem Simuka, instructs mother Africa to stand up and protect her resources from plundering by foreigners as it encourages Africa to make her children the heirs to her heritage.

> *"Africa,*
> *Simukauonekere.*
> *Mira panzvimbo vana vawane pekubata*
> *Simuka uchengetedze nhaka yevana, Africa!"*

Here Africa who is the mother of children is urged to keep safe her children's heritage. Mothers are the managers and keepers of home as affirmed by our proverb which says 'musha mukadzi' for a home to be a home it is because of the presence of a WOMAN. Without a woman, there is no home. Mothers take care of their children's health through their cooking of nutritious foods in the home.

Talking to a colleague, about the book by Batsirai Chigama, Chidora said, the voices collected in Chigama's collection are a reflection of the period under interrogation which even led to the Operation Restore Legacy of home, a military intervention that brought in the new administration in November 2017.

A voice in Memory Chirere's poem 'Pamhararano' (crossroads) from his debut Shona poetry collection, 'Bhuku Risina Basa: Nekuti Rakanyorwa Masikati' asks everyone talking ill about home that if all those that are clapping hands for the voice are silent, what else will the voice talk about?

> *"Kana vose vanondiomberera vanyarara*
> *vave kuda kunzwa zvimwe zvine musoro*
> *ndichataurei?"*

The voice further asks that if the poem that the voice is reciting, reading or writing has exposed all the bad about home, and made the voice the hero of exposing the ills about home, where else can it go and stay?

> *"Kana detembo rino rafumura nyika*

ndave gamba rokunongedza zvitadzo
ndichaenda kupi?"

The voice in the poem continues to introspect and point that home is where one was born in and the umbilical cord was interred.

Gather the Children is not a single voice but a collective in a dialogue with other voices produced before it which also were not happy with the state of affairs in the homeland whether perceived in the mind or in the physical or the spiritual. The poets dream and hope for a home of peace, unity and understanding though they differ on what home is but all agree on that wherever home is it should be a place of happiness.

References

Audrey Lindani Mutinhiri, Edmond Shonhiwa and Noreen Sadziwa, *Flowers of the Dry Season* (Forteworx Press, 2015)

Batsirai Chigama, *gather the children*, (Ntombekhaya, 2018)

Brian Chikwava, *Harare North* (Jonathan Cape, 2009)

Charles Mungoshi and Ignatius Mabasa, *Illuminations 25* (The Rathasker press, 2009)

David Mungoshi, Live Like an Artist, (Bhabhu Books, 2017)

Lazarus Sauti, *Nei?* (Royal Books, 2017)

Lilian Dube and Mgcini Nyoni, *Daybreak* (Poetry Bulawayo, 2010)

Memory Chirere, Bhuku Risina Basa:Nekuti Rakanyorwa Masikati, (Bhabhu Books, 2015)

Eppel explores 'unbelonging' in new work: Between the Lines
Beniah Munengwa

To be a person who lived on the other side of the fence always leaves one with a problem of binaries. One such man is John Eppel, a writer who finds himself in a category which fits many, the likes of David Coltart and Doris Lessing, who, however, find themselves belonging to neither side of the "racial" fence.

Just like Coltart, Eppel at one time found himself fighting on the side of the white man's forces. Afterwards, we locate these two figures attempting to shed off those shackles of racist and imperialist terms to being the eye that explores and cautions both good and bad in either racial grouping.

In them, we find a quest of belonging and an attempt to fit in, into African humanity with every inch of their bone and not be seen as savages, as reverse racism now puts it.

The content of Eppel's writing is that of a man who is in touch with the problems of either civilisation. He is a writer, who in an interview with Ambrose Musiyiwa, claimed to have been strongly influenced by Charles Dickens' focus on the marginalised people and he, himself, too has been marginalised, having had many of his manuscripts rejected by Zimbabwean publishing houses.

One of the works that relate to his claim of being overtly African is his latest offering, *White Man Walking*. The name White Man Walking is, however, not new, having been used by American writer, Ward Brehm, for the book, White Man Walking: An American Businessman's Spiritual Adventure in Africa.

In the new offering, Eppel explores the nuances of colonial and post-colonial existence in Zimbabwe. Some major recurring thematic concerns dealt with are the closeness to violence that the government is, when dealing with anyone who seems to go against it.

One notable feature is that all stories were written while former President Robert Mugabe was still in power. The story, Democracy at Work and at Play, underscores the deep-rootedness of Mugabeism, especially in rural communities. While the constitution-making process was supposed to be puritanical, the lack of accommodation of divergent thought and the underscored vision of trying to convert the Constitution into another version of craft that extends Mugabe's time in office takes charge.

Eppel, in an independent interview, highlighted: "My main concern in my prose is to ridicule greed, cruelty, self-righteousness and related vices like racism, sexism, jingoism, and homophobia."

With regard to his revelation, much of his stories pick up the strands that influence the way in which Zimbabwean governance and leadership unfolded.

He explains why he prefers to use satire in his writing saying: "I am under no illusion that my satires will make the slightest bit of difference, but nobody, not even those who are ashamed of nothing, likes to be laughed at."

Chiefly among Eppel's subjects of satire is the greed associated with the politician or his wife. Symbolising it was the recurrent question, "Where's my tub of Kentucky fries?"

In the short story, The Award Ceremony, instead of mourning the dead after a tragedy, the minister's obese wife finds herself only caring about her Kentucky fries.

On a deeper look, the way the politician's wife causes the suffering of innocent civilians and without feeling a sense of shame is synonymous with the bad girl tag associated with the then First Lady, Grace Mugabe.

In the era of Mugabeism, the probability that anybody would be working for the Central Intelligence Organisation was very high. Such is the case of Mr Abednego Dolobenj, a school teacher in the story, Profile of a School Teacher.

The outstanding story for me is NGO Games, primarily because it explores the template formulae in which non-governmental organisations go through in their day-to- day running. Blended with deep-set humour, Eppel portrays NGOs as organisations that thrive mainly on report writing and generation and less of any helpful initiatives.

This story falls under the same category as the author and poet's thoughts, that "international organisations will not help a white artist, no matter how poor," he is.

While the overall picture may portray Eppel's satire as overtly pointed to the system heads, one cannot ignore that some of it is pointed at the general public, who foolishly assume that they can unearth the roots of the system single-handedly. The end result, as shown in the stories, The Weight Loser and Sewage Pipe, where characters attempt to demonstrate against the system and end up molested by people on the lower end of the system.

Eppel's book stands as an independent project that is outstanding and refreshing on a different level, thanks to the meticulous input of the publisher. Thus in spite of a few errors, it is a book that I can proudly add onto my library.

This article was originally published in the NewsDay Issue of, 11, June 2019.

Title: White Man Walking
Author: John Eppel
Publisher: Mwanaka Media and Publishing (2018)
ISBN: 978-0-7974-9548-7

Confessions of a book reviewer and writer
Tanaka Chidora

Introduction

For almost two years now, I have been reviewing literary texts for *The Herald* (Zimbabwe's largest daily) and my own blog (www.litmindssite.wordpress.com). It's been a mixed experience for me which involved hunting down books whose authors were as elusive as the mythical Eldorado; or sometimes receiving poorly converted PDF versions of the authors' "latest" publications. For a reviewer living in Zimbabwe, buying a review copy every week whose cost was superior to what I would get for the review was an untenable choice. Then there was always this other book, from a zealous and self-published author (or one who had published with a publishing house that was set up specifically to publish that particular book) with missing words, a clichéd plot, an acquired taste… generally, a boring, half-done (sometimes quarter-done) read! My experiences as a reviewer have shown me that the future cannot be bright. I know the reading culture is in some ICU, but writers are also doing themselves a lot of disservice by not writing well, or by making their books difficult to get. This paper is therefore a laissez-faire collection of reflections based on my 2-year stint in book-reviewing circles. The general conclusion from these reflections is that marketing, editing and creativity need to be revamped for books to leave footprints even in this era where readers must be coaxed to actually read books.

Uncle Tich, Books and I

I grew up in the village with my parents and my siblings (Sue, Josy, Anne and, later towards the 2000s, Tawa). I was born in the 80s and started going to school in 1992. For my generation, especially those who grew up in the village, there was no pre-school. You just reached school-going age (7 years) without any pre-Grade One nurturing. Pre-school was merely a matter of going to the community centre (this one under the Musasa Tree, near the township) and eating porridge, this a product of some philanthropic interventions to make sure that village children did not succumb to kwashiorkor, whatever that was. By the way, going to school was also a matter of being able to touch your ear by stretching your hand above the dome of your head. Being able to pronounce 'Birth Certificate' was an added advantage. The rest was left to your Grade One teachers who really did a good job of making you pronounce the 26 letters of the alphabet by using a song about *manhanga* (pumpkins). I had a problem with the letter 'K', a problem that lasted a couple of months. I breezed through my Grade One without being able to read my school report. I would get to know my class position after getting home. Then my mother's facial expression would tell me if the report contained good news or not. It always contained good news.

My first free reading involved the book of Chronicles, which, in Shona translates to *Makoronike*. The Shona bible of old represented a reading hiccup for a naïve reader of my calibre, so the funny 'zv' and 'ch' in there provided a couple of hilarious moments for my mother who loved to eavesdrop on my reading.[1]

From Grade One to university, my parents, God bless them, trusted my work ethic so much that they practically left the choice of what to read, and when to read, to me. I don't remember them tyrannically dictating the homework-first-TV later rule to me that I see many kids enduring today. Of course, you might want to say TVs were not a common phenomenon in the village in those days. So find anything to use instead of TV. *Mahwani Touch*, bakery or *tsoro* if you want. Our parents practised a laissez-faire approach to education: I had to decide what I loved, and they had to provide the means (sometimes labouriously). Lots of times, I had to join them, either as father's *dhakaboy* (a colloquial term for someone who mixes mortar for the builder), or as mother's runner at the township market. During the cropping season, after helping in the fields, I had to look after our small herd of cattle. With such a busy schedule, novels still managed to find me. Of course, reading at

---

[1] *For 'zv', the old Shona bible only provided a funny looking sagging 'z', and for 'ch' there was only a lonely looking 'c'.*

the pastures was a traumatic experience, for the books that is. Many of them had mud splotches and dog ears to show off the experience of being read at the pastures.

By the time I completed my seventh grade at Mutya Primary School, I had already breezed my way through every popular Shona novel one could think of. My reading of these novels was necessitated by two things. First, Josy loved to unceremoniously insert long paragraphs of any Shona novel she would be reading at any given time into an everyday conversation. Imagine, you are having a conversation about invading Mbuya VaRusekeni's mango orchard, and Josy rattles up something from *Kutonhodzwa KwaChauruka* for effect. Only a perfect WhatsApp emoji can capture the confusion that would appear on our faces. So I took to reading every Shona novel that came my way. Some came as complete packages; others came with a couple of missing limbs, but the good thing about Shona novels of that time was that like Nigerian movies, getting into the story 25 pages later was no serious setback. The second reason was my late cousin, Innocent (may his soul rest in peace). This naughty fellow had a bookphobia of unimaginable proportions. So he would bring his Shona set books home and during bedtime, instruct me to read for him, a chapter per night. Of course, a couple of paragraphs later, he would be snoring loudly so that anyone who dared to listen from the outside would think that I was performing some incantations to the demonic approval of some dark force.

After sensing an invasion of her turf, Josy later migrated to English novels. However, I suspect that her affair with English novels was not a deep one because instead of citing whole paragraphs like what she used to do with the Shona novels, this time she confined herself to sudden citations of novel titles and their authors. For instance, during a game of bakery (I think that's the spelling; no one bothered to spell the names of games because games were meant to be played), she, from nowhere, announced, *Silent Journey from the East*. So I migrated as well, but unlike Josy, I actually wanted to read the contents of these novels.

Form 1 of course started with the usual: *Mpho's Search*; *Oliver Twist*; *Tunzi, the Faithful Shadow*; *Crossing the Boundary Fence* and so on. Then came Holly Meyers from the United States. She practically upgraded our Rukovo

Secondary School library and introduced a reading culture by making sure that every Form 1 pupil had a reading card. In the library, I stumbled upon the Nancy Drew and Hardy Boys series and loved them. I think I read 66 Hardy Boys novels and around 54 Nancy Drews. I usually worked at a rate of two novels per day. Even my English compositions became action-packed, reflecting the influence of America on a young village boy of my calibre.

Then my uncle, Uncle Tich, came to the village from boarding school. Uncle Tich represented what the village was not. He listened to foreign musicians, and usually whistled 'From the Distance' when absent-minded. This song remains a classic for me. There was something foreign and fresh about him that made me want to be his friend. He also brought Dambudzo Marechera (in books and in appearance), Mario Puzo, Robert Ludlum, Wilbur Smith, Jack Higgins, Frederick Forsythe, Eric van Lustbader, Sidney Sheldon, Ken Folliet, Louis L'Amour, James Hadley Chase and many other popular writers.

But the one who really invaded Uncle Tich's life was Marechera. Besides the unlimited collection of expletives that Uncle Tich used when angry or happy, he also began to exhibit behavioural traits that Marechera was famed for. For me, that was what set Uncle Tich apart. It drew me close to him and I became his disciple, reading his books and imitating his English. By the time I reached Form 4, I had read *The House of Hunger*, *Scrapiron Blues* and *Cemetery of Mind* and many other trend-setting Zimbabwean works. I had also read *The Great Gatsby* and many other literary works including *War and Peace*. I was the first, and I am sure the last, to borrow it from the school library. I still remember how I walked up and down the corridors with the book pressed to my chest. *War and Peace* is a voluminous affair and a Form 2 pupil must really be Marecherean to walk around with it.

Uncle Tich had a typewriter. He wrote his stories using that typewriter. I borrowed it from him to type my first story, 'The Mountain'. I deliberately lost it when I came to Harare. Uncle Tich has lost his stories too. He has also lost the Marecherean disposition that made him a rebel of sorts. Now he is all reserved and 'normal' but the linguistic dexterity is still there. A couple of weeks ago, I sent him a poem titled 'Life': "She led me to the house at the end of the street, and left her caresses on my face."[2] He added two lines about "dark voyeurs" peeping at us from the thick but perforated blanket of darkness, and I knew I still had my favourite uncle around.

Now I teach literature at the university. I have all these books in my head, but every time I rattle off some titles like Josy, I am met by blank faces. I don't know if the generation of learners we have now is different from ours, but the truth is that they no longer read these books like we used to. And some of these learners sometimes accost me on campus, or visit my Whatsapp and Facebook inboxes to tell me that they are writing some books. Really?

Hi, I am writing this book...

I started studying literature at 'A' Level. I remember that while I was waiting for my Ordinary Level results and herding cattle in the Chiriga hill, I was reading Mungoshi's *Walking Still*. There was a short story that caught my eye. 'The Little Wooden House in the Forest' has a dream-like flow and I decided to writer an experimental short story based on that. A week later, I wrote 'The Mountain', a short story in which a lover who lost his woman to tragic circumstances during a romantic trip to the mountains relives the episode over and over again until he decides to join her. I wrote the short story on some poor newsprint that had blotches here and there from mangoes, soup and *mazhanje*. The story came out well I think.

I wrote another one. This time inspired by Mungoshi's 'The Accident' in *Coming of the Dry Season*. This one was titled, 'The Announcer'. It features a man who was a runner for the 'most patriotic' (you understand why I used these quotes, right?) party in the country, calling people to the party's endless meetings, threatening those who chose to work and not go to the meetings with various forms of frightening things (like flogging at the party office and so on). He is involved in an accident during one of his rounds, and the atmosphere at the accident scene mimics the atmosphere in Mungoshi's 'The

---

[2] *This poem appears in my yet to be published collection, Because Sadness is Beautiful?*

Accident'. I later borrowed Uncle Tich's typewriter to type the two stories and hide them in my suitcase for safekeeping.

When the cream and blue-coloured ZUPCO chicken bus (and oh! Did I tell you that I am currently writing *Zupco Diaries*?) arduously transported me to Masvingo, to be transported by Mhunga and Sons Bus Service (it was some kind of relay) to Harare to start my A Level studies, I carried my short stories in my suitcase. Well, to be honest, it wasn't really a suitcase, but then that's a story for another day. I was supposed to carry out my studies at Harare High School in Mbare, but then I was told by some authority there that the number of O-passes I had scored was too modest and therefore I didn't qualify to study there. So by some dint of fortune I found myself at Mt Pleasant High School, studying Literature in English (for the first time in my life), Divinity and Geography.

I remember fishing out my two typewritten short stories to show them to a girl who had taken my fancy. She told me she loved them, but was honest enough to tell me that the same did not apply to how she related with me. It was quite heart-breaking (my first heartbreak I am sure) but I am glad I came out of it unscathed. The same cannot be said about the short stories though. I donated them as tissue paper to some denizens of Magamba Hostels who found it treasonous to use as tissue paper newspapers that had the face of the president emblazoned on them. Back then, the then president was always the headline. Nothing much has changed now.

The point I am trying to make is that I wrote two short stories that were inspired by stuff that I had read. We write because we read. To read is to intellectually invest in the art of writing.

So you have this chap who walks up to me and says, "Look, I am writing this book and I want you to check it out for me." And I am like, "Alright, let's have a look." By the way, this young chap does not know you do not just walk up to people and ask them to read your work. Reading other people's work is a job. I must be paid for my services. But I forgive this chap because he has this light in his eyes that shows that he is really serious. A perfunctory glance however shows that he is poorly mimicking so and so, so I ask him, "Have you read so and so's work?" He looks puzzled. He is probably asking himself why the heck I am asking such an irrelevant question. He says, "No, I haven't." "What about this other so and so?" "No". "What about...?" "No". The No's are so generously pronounced that I decide, remorselessly, to hand back the chap his book.

That's the kind of trouble I run into most of the time. I am now convinced that many writers, especially upcoming, from Zimbabwe, do not read each other's works. They do not read many works from beyond our borders either. Their culture of reading is so dead that what we write is also dead. So we have kids (both physically and metaphorically) thinking that they have written this big thing, but when you get to it you see that it is a poorly done parody of someone else's well-written book which the kid did not read. Sometimes, while reading someone's draft, I feel that if they read so and so's work they can actually improve their own. When I break the news to them, I sense the reluctance to read. The more careless ones take their work and disappear for good, only to surface with a Whatsapp message consisting of a poster that is inviting me to a book launch!

The older generation of writers must be looking at us with trepidation. What can the future hold when it is in the hands of these kids?

Then there is this one who hires editorial services with a launch date and venue already set...

In the Literature Today column of *The Herald* of 11 November 2016, Stanely Mushava wrote passionately concerning the downside (it also has an upside) of self-publishing. In a paragraph that lyrically captured what had been boiling in my heart for a very long time, Stanely wrote: "When one sees a novel, for example, in low-cost packaging, with a cliché, a tasteless bouquet of platitudes and contrived plots, they are bound to miss the good old days when the tradition was more highly esteemed from workflow to reception." I couldn't have said it better! I am a proofreader and editor. Both proofreading and editing demand rigorous, close and careful reading. In fact, both require the writer stay away from his/her script and let the proofreader and editor do their work. Professional proofreaders and editors do not work for free.

They are professionals who have reputations to protect. So when they start working on a script, they want to give it their best.

But they can't give it their best when an impatient writer is nagging them for the script a few days after submitting it for editing and proofreading. Some even give you the launch date to scare you into working fast. But what they are forgetting is that part of editorial work sometimes involves making radical changes to a story, hacking off huge tracts of it and suggesting additions that are almost tantamount to re-writing the story. So how on earth will you do that with a launch date and venue all set? As an editor, I may even suggest that the story is too poor to go out there and needs extensive and rigorous work and research. How are you going to do that with the launch date and venue already fixed?

I am also a literary critic and reviewer. I receive many copies for reviewing. The bulk of the copies I have received this year are products of self-publishing. Some have been successfully read by my wife (Mama JC) and myself. Others have messed up our appetite for reading right from the cover page! So we have left them to gather dust somewhere on the bookshelf. Others have had the misfortune of being in JC's crawling path and he has done a good job of matching their physical appearance with their technical shortcomings. Now there is a second one called Stephanie. Soon she will be crawling. So the danger is real.

Last year, I received a script from a certain fellow who thinks he has been called to write a motivational message for Zimbabwe, especially the Zimbabwe of 'new' dispensations (in poetry I prefer the phrase, 'new dispersion'). I perfunctorily glanced at it and concluded that it needed a generous portion of time and will on my part to exorcise it of obscurity. The chap did not have that amount of time; so he took his script elsewhere only to turn up three days later lugging two cases of books that could fill a modest bookshelf like mine. He was smiling. "Mr Chidora, may I present to you my first book!" I received a copy for "reviewing". Unfortunately, the book found itself in JC's path and . . . you know what he did, lol!

I think an honest reader pointed out the serious shortcomings of the book to the fellow because a few weeks later, after the euphoria of having published his first book had evaporated, he came back to me, repentant-like, and begged me to edit the 'published' book in preparation for the second edition. I told him I needed a soft copy. He promised to send it. That was it.

Now I hear the second edition is out although there is nothing "second edition" about it.

It is becoming difficult to find a book in Zimbabwe, written by my generation of writers, which you can read seamlessly without that jarring sensation that is provoked by misplaced words, punctuation errors and misspellings. It's really difficult. It's either our writers are not choosing professional editors or they are not giving the editors enough time. Or it might be because the self-publishing route has made writers escape the rigorous investment of time and money that real editing and proofreading require!

The solution to mediocrity is clear: as a writer you need professional and reputable editors. They will charge a fee and you must be ready to pay. They will take their time and you must wait. They will give you advice and you must heed it. That's the solution. This is part of what it takes to be a writer. It's not just a matter of putting pen to paper. There is more to writing.

If an editor gives you advice and you do not follow it, it's an insult to associate their name with your work. An editor has a reputation to protect because editing is a business. But it's not just the editor who has a reputation to protect; the writer also has a reputation to build. There are two kinds of reputation: good and bad. So as a writer you really need to invest into that process that builds a good reputation for you. The publication of a technically flawed book is, bluntly speaking, a waste of time. Once readers discover that you love wasting their time, you have lost them, sometimes for good.

A story with misplaced punctuation marks, grammatical errors and a serious disrespect for the traffic rules of words does not stand a chance of being read. It takes one bad book to soil a writer's reputation. Sometimes it's not just the reputation of the writer that is soiled but also the reputation of books in general. That's the truth! In this day and age when the hard-copy reading culture is waning, bad books must not, should not, see the light of day!

Everyone has a story to tell, but how it is told, how it is packaged, is as important as the story itself. My hope is that the self-publishing alternative that our writers, established and new, are embracing is also accompanied by proper publishing processes especially editing and proofreading. I am a proponent of democratic writing space, but I am not a proponent of mediocrity in the name of democratisation.

A word of caution: these accusations of mediocrity exclude Brian Chikwava's *Harare* North or Ken Saro Wiwa's *Sozaboy*. Readers can tell the difference between linguistic deficiency and art. *Harare North* and *Sozaboy* are art through and through. The narrators' bastardisation of English is intentional. But I can't say the same concerning some books that I received for reviewing this year. Maybe one day, after reading every well-written book on my bookshelf, I will turn my attention to these books just to have a good laugh. But for now, let me remain silent!

I have this book I want you to review…

Then there is this other chap who wants me to review their book. They know I run a blog, and a column in the local daily, and so having me review their book is good for business. So they decide to send me a review copy in the form of a PDF that comes on Whatsapp and must be downloaded using my data. The PDF is a poorly done affair: some chapters begin after acres of blank spaces; some words are illogically spaced as if Lucifer has appropriated the spaces between for his insidious tomfooleries. Then I must read the PDF on my phone, or coerce my young brother who has an assignment to work on to give me his laptop (I am the one sending you to school, remember?). The poor fellow has no option.

When I am lucky, I actually receive a hard copy to review. Sometimes it tells me if the future is bright or not. A book whose author has really invested time and money in is easy to tell. I know we are encouraged not to judge a book by its cover, but I usually do that. People do that. There is nothing you can do about it. The best you can do is create a good cover for your book. Then, while I am still evaluating my luck, I receive a Whatsapp message from the author who is enquiring if I have forgotten that the book costs RTGS50. "What?! You mean I was supposed to pay?" I ask, astonished. Then the chap stammers an answer, "Ummm, you see sir, it's like…you know…"

But wait until you hear news of a book being launched in town, and then nothing happening after the launch. The book is nowhere to be found. Not online. Not in the few bookshops in town. Not even on the author's person. The book was launched specifically to disappear. And the publisher… well, that one was set up specifically to publish that particular book! So there is no publisher to contact. And because no one is talking about the book, no one is saying it's good, no one confesses to having read it, you decide to let sleeping dogs lie.

Are you saying this because you studied Literature?

No! But that doesn't mean I should demand that good books be written.

In fact, let me confess how bad studying literature to PhD level is if you are thinking of becoming a writer.

I am widely regarded as a writer in many circles. Even my business card, blog site, Facebook page, Instagram page, Twitter handle and many other pages, state first and foremost, that I am a writer and literary critic. But my CV so far does not contain a single creative writing project. Rather, it contains a list of critical works.

For some time now, I have been plodding along in *Magamba Hostels: a memoir that is not a memoir*. And recently, I started *Zupco Diaries*. These diaries are twofold accounts of a commuter's experiences aboard a ZUPCO bus from February, 2019 to December, 2019, that is, if by December 2019 ZUPCO will still be operational. Things have a tendency of happening too fast in Zimbabwe. On 17 July, I wrote the following diary entry:

When they told me that Vanda was dead, I stared into space, unseeing, seeing only a movie reel of everything that was Vanda flashing before me, to stop abruptly at Vanda standing under the tower light with his friends, painting the air above him with crawling wafts of marijuana smoke, and saying to me, mudhara huyai mumbopuller mbijana ka. And I remember taking generous pulls, pulling and pulling and hearing voices in my head about me being the beloved of blah blah blah, and wondering how the River Jordan could contain the weight of such a revelation. I mean, the sandals, the dove and stuff. It's like you are sitting downstream and the Jordan suddenly decides to give you a dose of reality and you discover in its murderous tempest that being the beloved ain't kids play and all you can do is tuck your tail hurriedly between your legs and raise enough dust for the Jordan to be blinded. Later before going to sleep, Vanda sent me an app message and told me that the grade he had given me was from Malawi or somewhere of that sort. Then the following day, Vanda is gone. I mean, how do you balance that? Can someone please balance me?

The amount of creative exertion that I had to dispense to conjure those few words into life is short of extra-terrestrial. Sometimes, I perform self-diagnosis and conclude that I am suffering from a disease that is fashionable among writers – writer's block. But then I ask myself, *kuti mwana wekuMagaba angazwa zvinhu zvakadai here?*

My recent diagnosis has to do with schizophrenia. I think I live in many worlds. I have always lived in multiple worlds ever since the monolithic narrative of my village life was cut short by a Hardy Boys and Nancy Drew invasion, at which point I strove to see Chet Morton in his jalopy (whatever that was) munching a hamburger (whatever that was, again). It was no mean feat, especially when you were herding cattle atop the Chiriga hill to the south of Mutirikwi Dam.

Then fortune provided me with an aunt who whisked me away to the city, for the first time since my born day, to study A-Level. I woke up in Magamba Hostels in the morning to spend the day in Mt Pleasant. It was like crossing the boundary fence. Sometimes I ask myself, should I write about Magamba Hostels or my village? But even recreating my village is no mean feat. Many times I go there, I feel like Lucifer, like I am just passing by. This has been exacerbated by the recent *lantana camara* invasion that has turned the once familiar plains into unfamiliar spaces. So, I go back to Charles Mungoshi's 'If you don't stay angry and bitter for too long' in the hope of gleaning something that can help me write about my village in a more meaningful way.

The thing with being a literary critic and a writer is that the heightened and blatant self-consciousness that you wield as a literary critic keeps interfering with you every time you try to write. When I wrote 'The Mountain' soon after writing my O-Levels, I was an innocent young fellow with little experience of the world of books. Years later, after reading and critiquing many short stories from the likes of Anton Chekhov, Ernest Hemingway, Luis Bernado Honwana, Memory Chirere, NoViolet Bulawayo and others, I feel remorseless about making 'The Mountain' go through the trauma of wiping a patriotic citizen's backside. I do not regret losing the short story.

I am a writer, yes, because I have written some critical works, but right now my obsession with writing creatively has made me think that to be a writer is to be a novelist, a poet or a short story writer. As a critic, I have heard so much about what others say concerning so-and-so's work – the syntax, the themes, the worldview, the intention, etc – and I have even contributed my own share of such critical views by saying so-and-so should have written like this, or so-and-so failed to see that, or so-and-so could have depicted this phenomenon like this.

So, when I attempt to write creatively, I hear all these voices, mine included, laughing in the background at my failure to see this or that.

For example, if there is one character I have struggled with in *Magamba Hostels*, it's the hostel bully. This hostel bully, I tell myself, sometimes vacillates between being NoViolet Bulawayo's Bastard or Richard Wright's Bigger Thomas (before the crime).That's where the struggle comes in. I want a hostel bully who is fresh from the oven, someone never seen before except in my *Magamba Hostels*. I don't know if I am going to pull this off, but I will try.

Then there is this busload of theories that I have been using to critique other people's works: feminism, Afrocentricity, post-coloniality, queer theories, post-modernìsm, etc. it does not help that I teach Theories of Literature at university. All of them are clamouring for my attention and causing, in the process, a din that continuously saps my creative energies. The recipe of instructions on how to, and how not to, that sits before me destroys my impulsive creativity. The tyrannical voice of theory keeps taking my mind for a walk down corridors of theory when the only thing I want is to write my stories and not give a damn about what so-and-so said.

When the critic is also a writer, which identity, if I may ask, is central? Which one is tucked into the other? The truth is, when people read *Magamba Hostels* (that is, if I finally manage to lay down this critical garbage that is slowing me down), or *Zupco Diaries,* or the collection of poems that I submitted to a publisher recently (*Because Sadness is Beautiful?* is the title), I want them to understand me as a writer and not a critic, and when they read my critical works, I want them to understand me as a critic, because we can only give to criticism what belongs to criticism and to narrative what belongs to narrative.

Now do you see how I am in a quandary too, and that whatever I have said is not being said because I occupy an ivory tower of sorts but because I actually want to see my generation of writers reaching and surpassing the same heights that the older generation of writers reached!

Where to from here

I have often argued that there is nothing new under the sun every time someone came to me with the argument that I should write new things. But I think my argument basically sums a truth we need to accept. Whatever you are going to say, someone might have said it. So if that is the case, how do we circumvent the problem I highlighted earlier, the problem of mimicking poorly what others have written? By reading other writers, discovering how they have expressed what we want to express, and going a step further. Or we can create insaan soup. If you were once a bachelor like me you will probably know how it works. *Matemba, machunks, mazai* and *mufushwa*, all in one massive pot!

I have been told by an eminent writer, that my poetry vacillates between Hove and Marechera. This means it's not Marechera through and through, right? It's not Hove through and through, right? But the truth is these two are some of my best poets from Zimbabwe. So when I write there are things that they did with verse that find themselves in my work. I think that's how we create good literature (well, I am not saying mine is the next big thing). Recently, Rosa Tshuma's Zamani from *House of Stone* has been compared to Rushdie's Saleem Sinai in *Midnight's Children* and Charles Kinbote in Vladimir Nabokov's *Pale Fire*. But I think I can safely say there is evidence in *House of Stone* that Rosa Tshuma is a voracious reader, and that she might have read *Satanic Verses* and *Pale Fire*, but even though that might be the case, *House of Stone* is a stand-alone piece of work. Our works reflect the things/literatures that influence us, and these things/literatures serve to make us better writers. We have more advantages than the writers who wrote before us, because we have more work to read that is at our disposal than them. Lots of work! So the way forward is if my generation of writers become readers, read each other's work, read work from beyond our borders... a practice that will enable them to be aware of how far others have gone and the amount of creative investment that is needed if they are going to be like those writers or even better.

Writers also need to be prepared to invest in the editing of their work. No short cuts. Find reputable editors. At least two. Pay them. Editors do not read books for free. Give them time. Do not come up with the launch date and venue before the final, flawless product is out. Then after these two find a reputable proofreader.

Market your book. As an author, have a plan of how you want your book to get out there. Part of the plan includes review copies. You shouldn't be pestering me to send you Ecocash after giving me a review copy. Make noise about your book. Do everything in your power to make it available. Submit it for national awards even. Try to get it to CDU! Let it be known! Buy other writers' work. Talk about other writers' work on public fora. That way they will buy yours and talk about it.

Conclusion

Zimbabwean Literature, in all languages and genres, started well, on a high note actually. The generation that wrote during "those years of drought and hunger" of the colonial period did a commendable job.[3] We are looking here at the likes of Stanlake Samkange, Charles and David Mungoshi, Patrick Chakaipa, Paul Chidyausiku, Dambudzo Marechera, Musaemura Zimunya, Wilson Katiyo and so on. Successive generations of the likes of Chenjerai Hove, Tsitsi Dangarembga, Shimmer Chinodya, Alexander Kanengoni, Memory Chirere, Ignatius Mabasa, Petina Gappah, Chirikure Chirikure, Brian Chikwava, Virginia Phiri and so on have done a remarkable job. My own generation needs to keep the fire burning. And to do so, we need writers who read, writers who do not do shortcuts, writers who invest time and resources into the work, writers who market their work well. The time to misuse punctuation marks and commit silly grammatical errors is past. The time for clichéd plots is way past. So I am calling on my generation of writers to carry this burden of keeping the literature sector of Zimbabwe alive and healthy.

---

[3] I borrowed this phrase from the title of Musaemura Zimunya's critical volume, *Those Years of Drought and Hunger (1982)*.

Chinodya's Queues still mirrors Zim's problems 15 years later: Between the Lines

Beniah Munengwa

ZIMBABWE is currently experiencing queues, be it for fuel, cooking oil, gas and many other commodities.

Fifteen years ago, Weaver Press published the short story anthology, *Writing Still*, which carried a story by Zimbabwean literature legend Shimmer Chinodya titled Queues, which spoke to the reality of the time when "queues" had become part of life in the country.

This has become an enduring theme that speaks to a country battling an economic crisis for which queues for basic commodities are symptomatic.

Queues, a story which was written at the Caine Prize Workshop in Cape Town in 2003 depicts the life of a man that has "...been queuing up all his life" seeking friendship and tolerance but finding himself in "many a wrong queue, only to be told at the crammed garages of my fantasies that I am in the wrong lane, or to be turned away."

I met Chinodya at the recent launch of the book, Junctions, and that stirred my interest to revisit Walking Still, which was edited by Irene Staunton.

I re-read Queues in the context of the queues that I am seeing in my everyday life. The read could be depressing as one realises that independence came with a sense of despair and mistrust that pushed Zimbabwe to the brink.

The majority continues to sink in poverty while the powerful get richer and Chinodya observes that the "national cake was getting smaller, but suddenly everyone wanted a piece".

The story succinctly captures how things continue to deteriorate as the persona looks back with nostalgia to a time when his father could send all his three siblings to boarding school on a milkman's pay and how a loaf of bread cost 12 cents and a kilogramme of meat just a dollar. The standards of living are presented as having fallen.

In trying to rescue ourselves from the mess, Chinodya writes, "We borrowed and borrowed until we borrowed until we borrowed the word borrow."

Whilst the political and economic problems of post-independence Zimbabwe are what makes up the greater part of the story, how men and women relate in and outside unions is a gigantic feature of Chinodya's writings.

The extramarital relationship between Rudo and the iconic Clopas Wandai J Tichafa from Chinodya's classic book, Harvest of Thorns, unravels how wretched society has become as Clopas reflects on the degradation of social conditions, especially for the civil servant whose pay is eroded by inflation at the tick of the clock.

What does a man with a wife but without getting love from her do, if not to move on? But if he does, will he ever find peace in living away from his children?

Through their interchange, the deeper yearnings of a man's heart are revealed: "I told her I wanted a good woman to help me do that, that the best thing for a man was a good woman. A good, funny, honest woman. A woman to enjoy, to like, to love, to talk to, to laugh with, to devour, to feast on."

But, a strenuous relationship that takes a toll on one's psychological tank is always an undesirable one.

Society is presented as full of artificialities including theories that are mostly bar talk. "Perhaps the only 'isms we truly knew were chauvinism and sexism." These are what Chinodya picks as the real components of life for, although despised, they are what people practice.

Through Chinodya's iconic 2003 short story, you get to question why we express awe at the occurrence of queues and shortages in this country we call ours in this day and age. Literature through its power of documentation and reflection demonstrates that there's nothing new about any of the problems that we are facing as a nation and that, to hope will be to waste our time. Queues brushes shoulders with other interesting short stories like Memory Chirere's *Maize,* Charles Mungoshi's *The Sins of the Fathers* and many compact others.

This article was originally published in the News Day Issue of, 28, November 2018.

My Silent Grandmother
Tembi Charles

M y grandmother was a curious figure: a petite woman who visited occasionally, to spend time with us, of course, but also to sell all the doilies, bedspreads and clothes that she made from discarded factory offcuts. She needed the money to pay for school fees and to feed many grandchildren under her charge. My grandmother was not taken to words – she spent most of her time working. She was an industrious person who never liked too much talk. Open discussion of any topic was not her cup of tea. So that, when faced with unsavoury bits about someone, present or absent, she would sternly tell everyone to keep quiet. She said that words were very powerful; that once out from under the tongue there was no telling what would happen to them, for they took a life of their own. She believed that things should be kept under wraps, not discussed and aired, debated and turned around and round as people are wont to do. She said that, any bad talk about someone, even if it was a lie, would become truth. It was better to pay no attention to bad talk and to never, ever speak about other people. My grandmother said a secret was only a secret if one sat on it and then took it to their grave.

Even though my grandmother was a silent enigma, except for her sighs and grants, I loved her passionately. Her visits to our home in the city, were special. Much more special was the tasty wild fruit she brought from the village. Everything was packed in plastic packets or wrapped in brown paper and secured with colourful strings. Out came *umtshwankela, uxakuxaku*, and more; sweet wild fruit picked by my cousins back at the village. When one looked at those packets of goodies from home, tied up in old plastics and brown paper, which had been used over and over, one would not want to eat whatever came out of there, but oh, it was delicious. The wild fruit, the mealie-cobs, baked bread and scones. I devoured everything. The money she made from selling her wares was given the same treatment. It was housed in a sock, which was twisted several times, put in a plastic bag, twisted again and then put away safely under her breast.

Normally, my grandmother would arrive late in the afternoon. I would get back home from school and be pleasantly surprised to find her there. Of course, those days, most people never had telephones so there was no making of appointments and "booking" people as is done now. People just arrived – relatives never made known that there were coming. There was no letter; no word of mouth. Extended family just materialised at your door to stay for a day or two, a month or even a year. One was never meant to ask what visitors had brought and when they were leaving. Family was family and people stayed, and ate, and drank without paying for anything. It was one's duty to be hospitable and it was done out of love.

The interesting part of my grandmother's visits was the greeting ritual that happened as soon as my father arrived home from his butchery business. My mother would rush into my room which I shared with my grandmother during her visits and announce to my grandmother that my father had arrived. Custom did not allow my grandmother and my father to have eye contact. A son in law and mother in law should never set eyes on each other. It was taboo. Therefore, my grandmother would prepare for the greeting by pulling a shawl over her shoulders and tightening her *doekie*. My father would make his way towards my bedroom, from the living room where he would have had his tea whilst waiting for his dinner. He would position himself just outside our door, close enough to enable his voice to travel to where my grandmother was sitting. The door would be open just a little, and my father would begin:

Linjani salukazi? How are you all?
My grandmother would answer:
Hayi siphilile Gumede. We are all well Gumede.
And so it would go on:
Banjani abanye ekhaya, libatshiye bephila? How are others at home. Did you leave them alive?

Baphilile Gumede, baphilile sibili. They are all well Gumede, all very well.
Izulu? The rains?
Ah, komile qha Gumede, yindlala kuphela! Oh it is so so dry, hunger is coming.

Now and again my grandmother would lean over to steal glances at my father, and he would do the same. But they never actually made eye contact – custom did not allow it. Hiding behind doors and stealing glances at each other was the way it was done. It amused me to no end. It was difficult to reconcile that at home I was taught that eye contact with adults was rude, and yet my teachers at the Anglican missionary boarding school insisted that we do so because averting one's eyes meant that you were a shifty, deceitful person. If only they could witness this ritual between my father and my grandmother.

So that is how it was between my father and grandmother. I often wondered if they knew what each other's faces looked like, if for all these years they never really looked, really looked at each other. Years went by and my grandmother kept coming and going and I continued to witness their strange encounter. I would never have thought that a time would come when our two families would stop being close as a tongue is to saliva, that we would be divided by my mother's death and that my lovely, sweet, headworker of a grandmother would be called a witch. I would never have thought that my father, who had loved my grandmother so dearly would stand so far away from her and declare to all that she was a witch who had killed my mother!

The Poet's Revenge To No One Who Buys Poetry Books
Tendai R Mwanaka

The humans think they have just deleted you, dear poet. No one reads poetry anymore. I mean no one buys our poetry nonsense. Ask them to buy a copy and hear them running hard to find excuses, *"sorry I have financial commitments at home", "sorry I have a school grant to pay back", "sorry the government didn't increase my salary", "sorry my child has just died and I am burying her now"* (the last I checked he didn't have a child, and that's just last month ago!), *"sorry poetry vexes me"* (of course, you are pretty!). And the clever ones will lie to you they will buy a copy every end of every month until you are tired chasing them. I have done these chases and later realized even chasing a Zimbabwean girl for her heart's warm breath is child's play as compared to chasing this lot for their little scraps. You realize, later, they were just being polite, but no, they are not going to buy your poetry nonsense. There poet, you see where your revenge lies. No, they have enough money to buy poetry, where are they getting data bundles to stay online 24hrs a day, seven days a week, and 500days per year. Shut up you I-know-everything, I know your year has 365 days! This book only costs 15 bucks, not 365 days. The truth though resides in these lamessss excuses!

Start with the said government. Revenge for all those years you have tried to be a poet and pay tax and that government you pay taxes to doesn't do a single thing to help you to live like a poet. Mmm I wanted to say *like an artist*…and I was scared my big brother David Mungoshi will kick my butt for using the title of his collection of poetry! After all it's this same government to blame for not increasing the above reader's salary, yet you have been paying your taxes to the same government. That government has grants for farmers, for musicians, for industry, for social services, but not for the poet.

Don't sell your books, Poet. Stop doing books.

Instead mock that minister, mock that president, mock that governor, mock that councilor, the self-important senator. You are safe. That lot stopped reading poetry during Shakespeare's time, so don't even worry about using hidden poetic language. Use the ffff, the ssss words, strip them naked with your sassing words. No one is reading poetry remember so no one will be pissed by your use of these words. No rules apply on you.

Tell that professor fossil at your local university to shut the ffff up about poetry rules. You don't need that poetry education, who the fuck taught Shakespeare? After all, no one is buying poetry so what rules, to do what with them. Write like you have just awoken from the coma you entered before humans were even created and write so far into the future. I am serious, every poet knows the future, to millions and millions of years ahead of his time. Check the bible. Check the bhavagad-gita. Check the koran. Check the African bushman cave paintings. Who do you think wrote those books you are still using several mellenials later and take as the truth? How did the writer who wrote them come to know about you? Show me any other writing that has survived millennials that isn't poetry. Robert Duncan was right (I didn't say correct) in saying poetry resides in the office of God.

Reject everything (when I grow up, I will address this concept).

Ffffff with their grammar rules, ffff their metaphors, ffff similes, ffff images, ffff conventions, ffff alliteration, ffff whatever nonsense they harp about in those lit dead classrooms, making a career over dead poets whom they didn't support when they were alive. For goodness sake Dambudzo slept on park benches in Harare but see the scholarship the maggots have built around him. Where were they when he was struggling? They get thousands of dollars grants to study new African poetry, do they? No, they just copy what you the poet wrote poetically and put it into big, long winded, complex words, then garnish it by quoting one or two other fossil fuel scholar and there; see their bank accounts are honeyed as they go to sleep in the comfy of their leafy upscale homes in borrowdale, upper east, hamptons, sandton, south london, menlyn, ascot and you are left to rot in meru (I don't even know where that is), okay Chitungwiza, Soweto...

Or if one of those braveless little souls so called scholars really focuses on new African poetry and avoids New York Times indicted (I meant dictated but my mind failed to detect the word), African poetry, they will create solid and real scholarship on Africa but that will be the end of study of anything new in African poetry and those lazysss fossil scholars will copy that research for another 50 years until another brave braveless soul decides otherwise. You wonder why the Western Reader is still speaking orgasmically of Brutus, Achebe, Ngugi's Africa, etc… as if we are in the ffffcking 60s, or the watered down version of these you would find in the NYT Africa and The Guardian Newspaper whatnots. To think that less than 2 million American readers and one editor decides for a continent of over 1 billion people what Africa is, safely ensconced in their Western homes and offices. Dear poet, so when that professor fossil fuel start messing you about rules on your fb poetry posts tell him to shut the ffff up or go back to the classroom and boring grant writing. He has no hold over you. Zuckerberg has no University of Facebook, yet!

Write about that next door friend's wife you have been banging behind his back. Tell him in your poetry he doesn't read that you used your poetry to entice his wife into your arms. Don't worry, he doesn't read your poetry, and I bet the whole Mubvumira street's people don't read poetry, so they will never know about this. Write about that thief, the arsonist, that sodomising teacher, but don't go with this evident writing to the law man. You have no duty to a country that doesn't support its poets!

When they expect you to write socially or politically conscious poetry to quote in their politricking as if they are paying license fees for quoting you. Seriously if they were paying, the poet would be a rich middle class dude. Write about the trees, rivers, forests, mmm of high thighed trees, long rivered rivers, dark lingering banks, talk of dams that drips sweet scented enchanted waters, talk of the highs and lows of the rivers' waves, talk of the gorges, the forward thrusts of the river's waters, the sands oozing from your river. At least this oral exercise is beneficial to your broke sss psyche and body.

And when at your church they ask you to write a poem for the church, write it dear poet. No one reads poetry. No one buys poetry books. But know that they had never intended to pay you for that. That they would tell you that you are doing God's work. Ask yourself why they pay their parish priest, the pastors (here we are talking of those millionaire sssssholes) but they expect the poet to work for free because no one buys poetry books. Okay no one buys poetry books for real, that's why I wrote this diatribe. Write about DOG, write dog stuff, write about the dog's thread, write about chickens, about cats, write about sitting on the lawns, drinking cappuccino, swimming, cooking spinach, write about that middle class self-doubt boredom bullshit you find in White Western poetry these days. Write like everything is demanding an apology from you, as if you are responsible for killing everything that died since "In the beginning…" For sure the white man is guilty! And the black man is his hanging god now…

By all means go to the church and read your poem. They don't pay for poetry remember so who do you think you are trying to impress by writing serious stuff here. Not God. He knows everything already.

They say poetry vexes us but they still love and buy music, without worrying about the poetry in the songs. They say everyone is a poet, just like they say everyone is a singer, and if 7something billions of people are poets why the hell is the poet poor and the musician super rich. And if music is poetry on fire as they sometimes say why the hell is the poet excluded from the riches. He is the one who started the fire. So dear poet, do the Little Wayne on them next time they ask you to write them a poem they want to convert to music. *"Mememeeee me, me bitch, kikikiii, uwii humhum, nigger ha, ha dadada, di, ndindi sucker, fefefe, fefeku mullah baby ffff me, phew, grrrr, rrrr, motherfffer fffff, ssss, aaa, ffff you, Mememeee, me, me, I got money bitch, pfeeee…."* (I am sorry to the ZANU-PF's Pfeeerorists) I meant mumble, bumble, hark, gag, glut, groan, swore, shiver, puff, spit, whistle, laugh…, haloing rhythmically, like god ffffing Little When, like a bumble bee. Little When is the poet's answer to those ffffers who pay the musician but not the poet.

Why is everyone making money out of you but do not want to pay. Did you really expect me to know the answer?

Ask Zuckerberg. Paperbag created this facebook everyone is spending all their money on, so use this free book of the face to suckerpunch them with your poetry nonsense. They want to read a poem for free, and they will compliment you by liking your love nonsense poetry. Oh, how they like to read this love shit on facebook, and they tell you big black lies about your genius, *"wow"*, *"you are brilliant"*, *"OMG"*, *"you the best poet to ever come from Africa"*(going where), *"oh I have never read anything like that before"*. Yes, of course they have never read anything like that before. They stopped reading poetry books during Shakespeare's time and Suckerberg is only 32. If you think I am lying they stopped reading poetry books during Shakespeare's time, go and listen to Benedette Meyer on audio, in the late 70s speaking to Susan Howe, about Suck Town that will become Zuckerberg Town. She was complaining about readership and support from the establishment poets were not getting (anymore) in Uncle Trump's Towers. How about 50 years later in godforsaken dark Africa?

So instead of serving them the easy to read sweet love or inspirational diatribe they need to make themselves feel good with their nobodyness, rather write number poetry. Do Nicanor Parra on them, write anti-poetry and fuck with that Swedish kangaroo court that tells the whole world who is the best writer. They also do the no-Nobel on you, poet! Where is Nicanor's Nobel speech? If they could give it to the poetry in Bob ffffing Dylan groans, hoarse-shit voice moans, you wonder where is the Nobel speech for

....
....
....
....
............,

go ahead and fill up that space I left with our every year's near miss. As long as they are still alive, please don't provoke those that are with the maker. May God find mercy for their saddened hearts the Nobel Mafia burdened them with? You wonder how they came to read everything that's being written in over 10 000 languages and come to say this is the best writer in the world. It's like those other little sisies competitions like World Footballer of the year (Sorry to the Ronaldites rodents and Messites termites, it's you who crapped on that competition), Miss World beauty competition, Mr Universe (I wonder when they are going to give this to the trees…mmm aren't trees parts of this universe? And they are better people too!). Ffff Nobel, Fffff Guardian Fiction Prize, Fffff Caine Prize, Fffff Pulitzer prize, Fffff DAAD, ffff that dash dash Chapman prize (Chimpanzee), ffff every Literary gangster prize out there. They are not for the poet! I said do number poetry,

1, took 2, to turn 3, to
Ten, twenty metres to

40

4, took 5 to fight 6, eat
Thirty, pretty, eight, seven

Shiii, shut up professor fossil fuel. This is poetry for the lazy suckers who uses social network to read poetry they don't pay for. They still expect you to dish them a treat every day which they will use to court each other with, make babies on, and build their relationships on. Where is your payment, dear poet? Write that number poetry stuff and help promote population control. They have forgotten for them to be here its poetry that their fathers used to tame that wild Eve that their mum was. They forget that without poetry man is nothing, can't do a thing, and can't even tame the little wench. Go subvocative poet. I did that last year in Logbook Written by a Drifter,

Sub Vocative:
For Norman

Ooe uoi ooo oei eoea
Eoo uii iee ooe eeeio
Aae uioo oeei uiiioeo
Eeoo oiuea aeeiou eui
Aeeeo iouoi eoiuo aeeio

Eouioa
Eiii
Eoiuu
Aooiu
Eiii
Eouioa

Of course they are not going to pay you, so here is the last revenge for you dear poet. Don't stop writing poetry, just to spite them keep writing that nonsense. Write the poetry you want to write. Writing is for you, you need it. Don't worry your time will come soon into the future. The robots are coming to sit on their accountancy, engineering, clerical, fatssss managerial jobs and the safest career is of the creative, so stick to that now, dear poet. You are crazy if you think a robot will ever be capable of creating this diatribe.

But you want to live reasonably well like all these fffers now. So take time to do other things, learn other trades. I advise you to be a farmer. This is where you will ffff them better. Grow food for them and price it high. Its only food they won't find an excuse for not spending those facebook bundles for now. Let them do their facebook shit whilst you are busy watering your carrots, veggies, cereals (I am not talking of Cereal Ramapostponer). Its food here, and then price your foods double the usual price to compensate for your poetry they have been reading for free. You make them woo each other with your poetry so that they will create more humans, whom you will grow food for. Now, you can control them. You have the inside track to both food for the soul and food for the body. This is your Custer's last stand dear poet!

POETRY

THE SAVAGE HUNTER
Nicholas M. Mwanaka

When you explode your song
Way up to the clouds,
Very often paralleled by joy
Or when you Express your kingly nature
Your prey on the ground quiver with fear
Birds and reptiles, to name a few

When you beat your wings,
Making commanding noises,
In the azures skies,
Some earth's creature shakes to the marrow

Why do you devour your species,
And not your offsprings?
I wonder at your sincerity,
When at times you pretend to be innocent

You hover like an aeroplane
When hunting gently on the plains
And like an arrow you nosedive,
Before you mercilessly tear your victim.

First African Woman
Beniah Munengwa

All what she upheld
Was their very own,
Yes, their authentic self,

That we should now sue
Those who copy
her architecture,
For infringement of copyrights,
Pure acts of plagiarism.

Being the flag bearing race
For the cradle of mankind,
Look, the black geographical topsoil,
And her black complexion,
Cannot be just coincidental

But this is no longer the case
For my beautiful Africana woman,
The one who did not require
Horse hair to look good,
Or tonnes of powder
To enhance her Africanness

Those days when she was
 at the apex of the sugar
mountain of goodness,
When she did not sleep out
In revenge of her husband's endeavours

Leaving the babies lonely,

Crying all night long like hyenas
Only to drink from the
Contaminated breasts
with half milk, half alcohol and dagga
Tomorrow early morning,

Oh, Okay, I haven't forgotten
The new wave of empowerment,

Officed in farts
Clesirdia Nzorozwa

Before a knife slit a throat,
The fart was loud it cause a storm.
The office blew and bloomed in filth,
There was a donkey about to die of guilt.
My mind had a question so aloud it spoke!

"Who farted in the president's office,
Who caused the smoke?"

You dare think he blew his o-ring,
The soldiers will have your head.
That was conscience deep in thought!

My mind in question aloud it spoke!
"Who sit on that chair except for him, himself?
"It's his that explains why he never choked?"

The wolf in this sheep must hang!
Clesirdia Nzorozwa

A sheep with the fangs.
A woman among man.
Arrogance flows in its veins!

In violence the wolf rose!
Our mothers love flows in his?
Brotherly love dead in dreams!

A sheep on the outside
Within a selfish hungry wolf lives.
Our hope to see the light got buried within.
Faith got lost in change beliefs...

Buried its true self in propaganda.
In masses we bleated change will rain.
May your rule reign forever!

My blood brothers and sisters the wolf in this sheep must hang!

Fellow Comrade...
Patched army camouflage,
Saw less boots we still fight.
A loyal man never abandons his own!

Cows get no hay...
Yet they drive carts in this scorching sun.
It Stewed, grilled and milked them till blood dripped from its breasts.

A foreigner to ruin his own he is!
A traitor to sell his own he is!

A coxswain in a sinking ship he is!
Should we die loyal to this dishonoured soul?

My fellow comrades the wolf in this ship must hang!

Unknown Citizen...
My pockets got admitted...
Its been vomiting 15cents...
A sickness the bankers can't cure!

I sweat more in this heat...
My job is more than the salary
A donkey I am...
Worthless, yes but we deserve more a penny.
The backbone just sank in deep into this rotten flesh.
Dust is all these sweaty hands ever held between my shadow and poverty!

Broken and bruised is mother
She wails *"my blind pure sheep drown in confusion who shall save them?"*

We are already dead man walking,
The peasants crowned king a knight on a forgotten quest.
The guillotine will serve its dark heart well!

What good is a fisherman with a fishing hook in a dead sea?
Will these poisonous toads in my basket make a perfect meal?
What a blessing it is to never be born into this dead land!

Citizens the wolf in this sheep must hang!

Traditional healer...
Lots can be casted.
The fallen and the gods can be trusted!

Whatever you sow you reap.

A toast to the blinded gods!
We still find strength caress this deteriorating, forsaken land.
Let's sing kumbaya!
The song of our fallen,
Who were shot dead for no reason!

The gods of this land shall hang in shame.
We as a people if we are not careful,
We shall be slapped with failure in public.
Hear me blind men, the wolf in this sheep must hang!

The begging sheep...
Torn wool, no one notices us...
Wait!
Can you reason with a hungry man,
Man so hungry for power he forgets his countryman?
Countryman who brought him to this patched worn out times we are now living in!

A fool can only fool fools!
Let's not point fingers and play the blame game.
Let's not say we were blind even the blind could foresee these future events!

Let's not say it was the excitement to be living in a barnyard under the rule of our own.
Let's open our hearts more, play less attention to the noise...

Now a burnyard the fire shall burn us all to ashes!

Silence. ⋯⋯.......
A small shaking voice..
Your own is never your own till they become God's own!

Your blood is never your blood till they become our ancestors blood!

Priest...
The wolf in this sheep must live.
Live to confess its deeds.
Live to be baptised by the hand of karma.
Live to be swallowed by the hollows.
Who are we to take another's life?
Are we not brothers even if it was born from a destruction demon?
The one born from wisdom and knowledge I pray he finds us!

A tiny voice...
Is there such thing as a good devil?
It swallowed its own!
What good is a lion among buffalos?
"The wolf in this sheep must hang!"

Silence...
Prejudices!
It's Not guilty!
Have Mercy!

The rising voices
Hang the sheep with the fangs!
Must hang hang hang!
The wolf in this sheep!
Must hang hang hang!
The lies in its speech!
Must hang hang hang!

Slaughter House
Clesirdia Nzorozwa

Sweet hay,
Milk my breasts dry.
Feta cheese.
Million in one,
You are never satisfied.

My whole being in a bottle.
You have *"a million ways to milk me"*
Partly Inside am mooing.
You have *"so many ways to make me feel less human"*_

Why does it feel like you are taking me straight to the slaughter.
Slaughter house!
My love for you is my weakness too,
You just taking advantage.

Your love is haunted,
I bet you have hanged hearts by the throat, slaughtered emotion by the
sword.
Take me to my tomb,
There I will lay alone!

Our home feels like an abattoir.
He makes me feel like a piece of meat.
Turn me to stew,
Call me biltong boo!
A thousand pies for you fool!
Protruding belly *"Billy the Pig!"*

If I muffle *"you sold a pig to a carnivorous!"*

Mother would say to keep silent or the world will cage me in gossips.
If I whisper *"I am dying slowly, this man controls me"*
Father would roar a man controls your world, yours died on the day you said
I do, no complaining die in your silence or the elders will say you are poison.

MEETING AN OLD FRIEND:
Kabelo Sithole

"The sky is falling." said he.
 "I wake up springing!" I said.

"The suicide rate is souring,
Please don't be a statistic." He, tragically, said.

 "At noon I write poetry to the sun;
Once you were God, now you are God's handy work!" said I.

He asked, "Are you happy?
You've lost a few around the belly."

 "I get by chilly nights in Gweru Musing over the moon,
 with a glass full of stars where my milk used to be." I replied.

Poisoned
Michael White

Sweet was it on the palate.
Something of a balanced mixture and texture of elements whose chemistry, complex and perplexing.
Stinging it was as it went up my temple than it did to my stomach.
Sweat droplets found their place on my forehead and immediately my senses began failing.
Slowly but effectively the poison found its way to my core.
Sensations unaccountable overwhelmed me manifesting the inherent vices.
Severe convulsions soon followed, the eyes were failing and the last sight they captured were scattered capsules labeled jealous.

FYI: It all starts when you get into bed, facing the ceiling with the lights out. Stream of consciousness.

R.T.G.S.
Mandhla A Mavolwane

Restoration of the legacy
Rescue the people from tyranny
Robin Hood with a crocodile smile
Robbing the hood with a smile.

Taxation for the common man
To pay a debt that is unknown
Tears are wiped out like the fifteen billion
The suffering is increasing like inflation.

"Give us a chance"
"Get in line with our stance"
Greedy bastards fart corruption
Grenades are thrown for any opposition.

Signing phantom investments
Sanity is questionable in parliament
Senile veterans are allergic to retirement
Save us from the pools of unemployment.

Head or Tail?
Mandhla A Mavolwane

A coin is tossed
Head or Tail?
A mind blowing rescue
Ululations and whistles
The old rooster finally shed its feathers,
But it forgot to shave its conscience.
The July winter marked its return.

A coin is tossed
Head or Tail?
A new vessel is rising like an erection
High hopes and aspiration
The future is sweet with perfection,
But it failed like a bank transaction.
The July winter brought perspiration.

A coin is being tossed
The common man farts in darkness
The old rooster barks promises.
A vessel is always making noises.
Head or Tail?
The old or loud?

True Lies
Mandhla A Mavolwane

You put a spell on me
I cannot give you the world,
But I'll hold onto you like a magnet.
They may call us names,
In our little garden
We are Adam and Eve
Our love is forbidden.

We battle against reality
Our union is filled with vanity
Our tongues twirl like a hoollahoop.
I know most of your fears,
I don't tell you mine
Because you won't feel safe anymore.

I want to tell you the truth,
I will only tell you that I love you
And that way you won't leave me.
My fear of trust is alarming
But baby enjoy this special moment with me.

In the name of the Father
Osman Shato Mbindi

Look!
Here they are
In the paradise of Babylon,
Fervently exorcising fabricated
Sea demons,
Deodorizing Jezebel's stinky breath
From their gold bought loved ones
Brought as reinforced concrete
For a hoodwinked sky scrapper,
Sucking the nectar
Of the drooping flaccid flowers
To ravenously feed their egos.
So, please!
Call the clan
And let's hastily brew the fermented queen
And chase away the lurking evil
Owl pouncing, claw hunting
And devouring the black souls
From our cleansed land.

The Draconian Crown
Osman Shato Mbindi

Amid the thick, still night
Jet –black,
I was puzzled
Grossly irritated
Then heartbroken,
By the deafening shrill screams
Of my clay people-my blood
Then I peeped through;
The lonesome old squashed;
Rectangular window
And saw them harshly strapped;
On a brown cactus
By a razor blade barbed wire
Across their withered
Roaring bellies,
While the red depressed drops oozed
Mixed with orphaned tears
Quenching the smouldering black soils
As I helplessly stared,
Watching their ash white
Cracked lips,
Bulging dry eyes,
Gazing desperately up
The bloody iron
Draconian crown

Dead dad
Osman Shato Mbindi

Once upon a time,
I dwelt under the leaking chalky roofs
Of the bruised ghetto of old Magwegwe
With my corrugated skinned
Broke dad,
Who came home like the Sahara rains
Sometimes in the witching hours
Sometimes never like the broken love vows,
Then my enemy;
Gweshegweshe's black scotch cart
With its loud hooter
Which horned, blasting every eardrum
Close by,
Summoning him like an evil spirit
As he vaporized into thin air
Like the dream of a well fed pauper
Only to return
Liquor drenched and soaked
Staggering blindly,
Stumbling
Falling
Uttering gibberish
And getting up…
To resume his journey to the cockroach house
Mother would be roasted by the landlady
Stung by her venomous scorpion nouns
And thunder slapped by harsh verbs
But this oversized dressed man,
Would thud on the bed;
Heavily, like a bag of cement

And then die....
Then came Monday
And the ghost game
The dew game
Continued as usual.

Ndakada moyo
naTinashe Muchuri

Handina kuona chiso chake chinaku
Kana tuswiti pamatama ake, kwete!

Handina kuona chipfuva chinotamba ngoma yeJerusarema
Kana mazamu ake anenge shongwe , aiwa!

Handina kuona chimiro chake chakaurungana sehari yamhizha
Kana kutsvedzerera kweganda nekupfava kwaro sedufu, hwava!

Ndakada moyo wake wapfava kunge donje
Ndakada moyo wake murefu kunge rwizi rurefu
Moyo unozvonyongoka uchinzvenga zvinetso nezvigumbuso
Moyo usina chinamira

Her heart took me away
Tinashe Muchuri
Translation into English by Tinashe Muchuri

It is not her beautiful face I saw
nor is it the dimples on her cheeks, no!

It is not her chest with breasts gyrating like they are dancing to the Jerusarema drum
nor her arrow like breast pointing to me, no!

It is not her beautifully built body like a champion potter's clay pot
nor the smoothness of her ripen *dufu* fruit like skin, no!

I loved her heart that is as soft as cotton wool
I loved her heart that is patient like a long river piercing through soft stone
Her heart that meanders evading challenges and angering spirits along
An unstained heart

Vanhu vanhasi here!
naTinashe Muchuri

Kungopa basa meso
Nzeve dzichitsinhira
Kunge vakadzi vanojijana paduri.

Kungofuratidza moyo
Fungwa dzichifonyokera
Sevaya vapirana makotsi muwanano

Ungavadii vanhu vanhasi
Ivo vachairi vemakombi
Kana mahwindi acho nhai
Panofa wavo ungapamira!
Chero une chivindi chemvumba,
Unonyepa!
Hazvidi muromo, ndezvenzeve.

Zuro zvandakanga mate mukanwa
Paya madzimai ekereke oimba
Zviya vachiti Mai Maria Mumureverere
Ndipo pakati chimwe chikomana chitsvuku chakadhakwa nyamwi
Diti rakanzi fenenga ndokusheedzera choti,
'Pamusoroi vekereke.
Pano hapana zvokurevererana.
Uyu haazi wenyu uyu, ndewedu.
Mukamureverera anomuka ngozi.
Siyai isu timuitire zvaakasarudza kuita achiri mupenyu.
Kwedu hakurevererwi naMai Maria.
Endei zvenyu mundovata makadekera.
Pano hapana chenyu, ndezvedu.'

63

Nemiswe yakapetwa pakati pamakumbo takakwesvaira tobuda.

People of today!
Tinashe Muchuri
Translation into English by Tinashe Muchuri

My eyes get stuck
Ears following behind
As women taking turns with pestles in a mortar

You just turn your heart away
With mind in turmoil
As those in marriage separation.

What can you say to people of today?
I mean the kombi drivers
and their kombi assistants
When one of them departs earth
Even if you are brave like a mvumba
You can't!
It is not for words but ears.

Yesterday I got awestruck
When the church women started singing
'Mai Maria Intercede for him'
Then a light brown drunk young man stood,
With chest raised high and said,
'I am sorry for you church people.
This man lying here in there is not yours, he is ours.
If you intercede for him, he will come back as an avenging spirit.
Give us time to do for him what he chose to do when he was still living.
Where we come from Mai Maria cannot intercede for us.

Go and sleep in peace.
This event belongs to us, please leave him to us.'

With tails between our legs we all marched out.

Withering Home
Trust Mauyasva

We walk on the predator's tongue
a city almost swallowed by a beast
caved and walled in sharp canines
a bite problem is the very least

As some sink deep in that venom
hopes for survival slowly slip away
trust fades, everyone a capable enemy
we pray, God help us see a way

Bundled up in, in pure desperation
if it is not killing, we have no care
I will rather see your tears than starve
I fear truth giving me courage for any dare

fight or balance just do not be swallowed
stuck in that belly there is no way back
we see evil around and sin differently
who is to judge as despairs rises a stack

This Thing Called evoL
Trust Mauyasva

feeding on my strength I wear and tear
watching my whole self fall off prey
I stare into the cold eyes that instil hate
each breath being an attempt to survive the day

all of me struggles with mere acceptance
the purity of cruelty rising in my Achilles' heel
planted in the same old disregard, unremorseful
continually I am bruised for showing how I feel

in a new fade the old spots still resurface
the same sting nurtured oozes and we morph
time travelling in the present to the origins of conflict
empathy and reason distant, stuck far off

at present night sleep reaches for elixir status
held together for these few breaths I am subliminal
cutting words over my memory to rewrite the past
for if I had known I would have kept it at minimal

Chasing Royalty
Trust Mauyasva

You are a beauty and quite aware of it
drawing me in with those pretty eyes and lips,
a near perfect captivating breathing artwork.
sadly some visions haze beyond your hips.

I would want you to step in my position
in vision, visualizing your concealed interior
perceive that intense glow obscure in you
agnise your salience, refrain from feeling inferior.

I long to really show you your true worth
get you away from empty smiles spewing fibs
have me levitate you softly into felicity,
revere you as royalty nurtured from my ribs.

my unfeigned love for you stenciled in rock
more than Queen, a throne making man royalty
i give you my ear like words from the scriptures
babe, be my sub religion i devote to with loyalty.

Children in the stones
Troy Da Costa

There are children in the stones
She said to me
But I did not understand
So I went to the water
The pool at the edge
Deep and blue in a hole that never ended

And here was the beauty we all desire
Serenity for lost and weary souls
Here the tears filled the pool
But words filled the flagrant air
Her words each one more disturbing than the next

I could not live with this riddle
Even in a place as intoxicating as this
So I moved to where the people were still like petals
Dreamers and believers
Clueless and confused
They should have been building great structures
And painting beautiful pictures or writing tales of magnitude
Instead they were set at all the endeavours they could've never hoped to
master

To the East
Finally, I stood at the bottom of a cliff
The granite glistening in the sun
The emptiness tore at my senses
I screamed at the wall
Until the rocks came down and I began to cry
There are children in the stones I heard her say

And they will never be free.

Tear Drop Diamonds
Troy Da Costa

A tear dropped on the widow's cheek
Like a diamond in the moonlight
A precious gift from her soul
To the one she used to love

So, he held her in his hidden arms
Bathed her in his darkness
And whispered softly on the wind
Like he wasn't there:

Hush now my loving child
Let me take your pain away
Let me hold you in my hidden arms
Until night becomes another day.

The Wheel of Clay
Troy Da Costa

We walk between the rows
In this godless place
And touch the ground with our bare feet
Where the bad thing grows

Among the weeds we plough and sow
Bound to this land's will
Upon a circle made of clay
Where the bad things grow

And the wheel it turns as the river flows
Its waters tainted pink
Burning in the brightly sun
Where the bad thing grows

From the sky the lead falls like snow
Into graves ten feet deep
Where soldiers on their wooden legs
Do the things they've always done
And will always do again

Die they must from crow to crow
Those helpless little boys
And spread their hearts into the dust
Where the bad things grow

THE OTHER SIDE OF THE COIN
Andrew Huje

Blistered skin and a torn muscle
Of a wrinkled mind, locks a thousand cries
Within the emptiness of days
On the other side of the coin:
What a day without its morrow,
And what happiness is without sorrow?
Glorious today tossed may fall a blackened day tomorrow:
Shortage, robbing, prevarication;
The Messiah is not, the Messiah is sought;
Under dusty carpets of the rich men mansions,
But this is the other side of the coin;
It is a horrified blankness, filled with empty words,
Where are we? Big, bigger, biggest?
Or small, smaller, smallest?
The smallest can be big but not biggest;
The other side of the story:
It is sadness beyond measure;
Sad stories of the uncertainty of it all!
What a day without tomorrow,
But what if it dawns evil in the morning
To milk the energy of other souls
Away, drifting apart like broken joints?
The old man lived well, but I in curses.
Why now when yesterday was there?
A'int thou hast been the black cowpea
That tinted good with evil?
Are you not black painted into a rainbow?
The bolt cutter for a mad, cleaning squad
Of the night?
There is the head and there is the tail.

What a day is without tomorrow!

I TOOK A BUS
Andrew Huje

I cough out fumes of burning skirts
Of my mother's dress;
She is dead, a ghostly being;
Wilting flowers to resurrect maybe.
Until then, I shall take a bus
And awake in a different womb;
I shan't milk you dry foster breast -
You are dear to your babes,
It's just that I am a babe in the woods
My blackened eyes embrace no light,
My mother is a burnt stub
Always harkens back to a lost day
And now the future is orphaned.
I left my mother's ash in the cold winter night;
I took a bus away from home!

MIDNIGHT PATROL
Andrew Huje

Where are you my soul?
Where did you run to, my undying essence?
Pocketing yourself in peaceful deep worlds
And watching the drama unveil.
I am weak, am I not?
Fought, am I not?
I stammer in times of chaos
Because I am empty inside.
Who shall speak your language if I am taken?
Taken from the battlefield and hidden in women's apparel.
Maybe time is not, maybe 't shan't be;
Fly into dark patches above and coil in absolute kingdom's beauty
And leave the dying me in the hands of a praying child
Whose words sail in the beauty of their innocence;
Watch me succumb to my end in your absence.
Where are you my favourite space?
Will we return to the fairness of days?
Blood and tear sunk within skins of unity.
Who ransacked the bag of my sweet dreams!

Angelic beings patrol at midnight,
Who shall be awake? No more fights, no war;
Just chaos before daybreak.

that stain
Jabulani Mzinyathi

that dementia displayed
at home and also abroad
the bragging long done
those degrees in violence

that stubborn stain on our minds
with what detergent or stain remover
will we wash or wish it away

taking refuge behind fingers
gratuitous dispensing of violence
kindergarten stories of self defence
the illgotten fake doctorate exposed

so take heed
Jabulani Mzinyathi

save a thought for the arts
there will be that ant voice
sounding those ominous warnings
ignore that ant voice to your demise

find time for the poets
the playwrights tell the stories
go see what the sculptors offer
the singers, the players of instruments

save a thought for the artists
those mirrors of societal concerns
that self glorification avoid
that mindless deification avoid

lessons in humility espouse
that relationship between fish and water
listen, the prophets speak still
your welcome never over-stay

the same dog
Jabulani Mzinyathi

with sycophantic dispositions
now they fall over each other

some turn to blasphemy
singing those empty praises

mere mortals are still deified
and they gobble the garbage

and then push comes to shove
they abandon the sinking ship

exposing those sycophantic tendencies
soon they may rename even rivers

MY FATHER'S BIRTHMARK
Prosper Kavunika

I was told I was born in the rainy season
In our small house which I grew up calling my mansion
In the dead of the night my mother cried out in agony
Her screams reached villages of far distances
The roaring thunderstorms and the flashing lighting accompanied her
screams
The coincidence in the occurrence of the thunder bolts and the eruptions of
her screams,
sent shockwaves to by standers
The moon hid behind the heavy dark clouds
Leaving much reliance on the flashes of the lightning to direct the way
My father made big and heavy dashes fetching firewood
With water dripping from his wet afro, soaking his entire body
Shaking and unsteady, his hands shiver because of fear and anxiety
Pacing up and down in the rain, he hoped for the best
Prayers and meditation, fellow women made at a distance
A well versed grey haired lady calmly prepared for my arrival
Even though the screams kept growing louder
My father moved closer and tightly held my mother's hands
Moments later the storm calmed and so did the screams
That is when I made my first gasp of air
My first burst of cry made many to jubilate
Unknowingly my father had lost one of his finger in the process
That is how he got that mark on his hand during my birth
My father's birthmark

DUAL CITIZEN
Prosper Kavunika

Once we were a blooming flower
Bright and colorful we stood tall
Only to be pruned and our petals scattered by the harsh hands of time
Some were blown away by the winds
Others were washed off by the waters
Those that were left behind were executed by the slasher
In different directions we were plucked off our bud
In different locations we found habitat

My body is here yet my soul is somewhere
My shadow is next to me yet my mind is set afar
My voice is heard here yet my hopes lay yonder

Each time I sit in the hazy gardens of Fort Hare
I always see myself pacing through the streets of Harare
As I gaze at the sky scrapers of Tokyo
Deep down in my thoughts I see my herd grazing in our fields of Mtoko
The scent of food in the fascinating kitchens of Beijing
Reminds me of the food of my grandmother in her muddy kitchen in Binga
The tranquil residents of Dar-es-salam "the abode of peace"
Is just a reflection of my people of Dangamvura
The thicket bushes of Bujumbura makes me yearn to take my dogs for a hunt
in ours of Mukumbura
The chill that blankets my body as I seek asylum in Canada
is totally different from the warmth in my home Karanda
The busy streets of Mbabane
Are similar to those of ours in Mbare
Moscow is snowy, Mazoe is golden
The distance between Quito and Gutu is lengthy
Ottawa and Mutawatawa are set apart by days

Lisbon and Lupane are of diverse cultures
I am a dual citizen.

Borrowed time
Nicole Vimbai Kazembe

We are on borrowed time,
So let's make this count.
We test how far our hearts can go
Until they can take no more.

Love me now
Until the break of dawn
Then when the sun comes out,
We know our time is up
Because we are on borrowed time.

Screaming Eyes
Nicole Vimbai Kazembe

Looking into your eyes,
I see you are full of belies.
They show all your denies
And tell of your demise.
They are screaming eyes.

You don't have to comply
To what society dictates
Because only you it hurts,
Trying to convert and divert you
From who you are.

You see, outside you are the world,
You have it all,
The money, power and the gold.
But my dear, I can see it's a facade
Because your eyes are telling.
Your inside has twirled,
Now you continue to swirl and swirl,
All l see are screaming eyes.

Screaming Eyes,
that want to say goodbye.
Screaming Eyes,
that want to close,
an end they have seen enough.
Screaming Eyes,
that want to let it go
and rest.

Don't sleep beside me,
Dark thoughts haunt me,
Especially in the night,
Thoughts of harm,
Harming whoever is in my way,
Harming whoever is close to me.

Dark thoughts haunt me,
Since the day he 1st touched me,
He was supposed to be my brother,
father, uncle.
I looked up to him, I trusted him.
He touched me, took my innocence
Before I even knew l was innocent,
Before l could spell the word innocent.

Don't sleep beside me,
Because in the dark it's only his face l see
And l want to harm him like he did me.
He took away my pride,
my confidence, my esteem.

I sometimes think of how l will batter him,
Throttle and slit his throat.
Please don't sleep beside me,
Because I don't want to hurt you,
I value you too much
To see me in my state of aggression,
When I live my fantasies while l sleep.
You are the only man l ever let in after my ordeal.

Don't sleep beside me,
I love you.

WANDERING THE STREETS
Pardon Sikula Moyo

I've been wandering all over
The streets of a dictionary,
Strolling cross the avenues
Of syntax and phonetics,

I found nude words lying idle,
I harnessed, and dressed them
With a poetic gown and crown
To water the ideas of my mind,

I roved past people's corridors,
A crude word slipped into my ear,
I covered it with a poetic garment
To dress the nudity of their minds.

THE FADING MOON
Pardon Sikula Moyo

One of those lonely nights…
We, coiled in the moonlight,

The moon shined a little bright
Shadows slowly engulfed light,

Foreshadowing the morning plight
The wind blew violin left and right,

Overwhelming darkness evoked fright
Our hair tickled escalating to fist fights,

The fights provoked dust like dynamites
Dancing in the dust with tightened tights,

We fought, furious fights without any flight
We hid in yonder cites far beyond their sight,

It all over smelt like the past days of genocides
Like tree leaves falling on grounds, we fell in eights.

THE FEMALE VERSION
Ruvimbo Mafukidze

Some have the preferred model bodies slick and slender
There are those who always add a pinch of salt to the milk
Always advising on taking vitamins to add some steak on bone,
Others have an extra pinch of sand and appear to be so curvy and heavy
Their structures are praised but others will always advise on losing a pound
or two,
Some appreciate her beauty but some always notice dents which need some
make up
Nevertheless light or dark skinned you compliment the toppings on the ice-
cream
Cherry, chocolate, peppermint or sprinkles you always pop out most,
Marvelous creations the chocolate we definitely cannot live without
This riddle lays idle unsolved for I fail to get the hidden solution,
Miss a period in your mother's house, an application for complications
Miss a period at your husband's house, an application for celebrations
Notice your flows at your mother's house get an applaud for good behavior
Notice your flows at your husband's house get more calls on his cheating
behavior
A woman in this era personified as a two headed Janus who remains the
same either way
Choosing the face to stare at once does not necessarily mean that the other
face is imperfect
For it is a sacred figure and a piece of art which definitely was performed and
created by love
Keeping in mind that it is a perfect and actual make so beautiful after the
creation of Adam
A piece of steak that is preferred for its tenderness and even disliked for the
same reason
In such a world where the burden is too much to bear, there is a need for
emancipation

The war my fellow women is fighting leaves one in a deep mess of confusion
Trying to figure out which is which, upside or the other way round
As being unique gets you labeled as nothing other than weird
Following suit like others now gets you insane labeled
As you follow the direction of where the wind blows
I wonder and ponder if we are being misunderstood
Is it because we are the female version or we are women?

RIP CHARLES MUNGOSHI
Ruvimbo Mafukidze

Cherishing the incredibility in your art journey is all we are with left
Having known that one day the big tree would collapse being such a threat
An experience which tortures us all the way is realizing a legend is lost
Rendering the missing chapter such an impossible task in the book of art
Leasing tear pumps becomes a uniform to us all whom you have ripped a heart
Enduring the pain gives us no option for we could depend on your part
Sorrow strikes millions of souls in the whole wide nation and its borders abroad

Much appreciation to your works which enriched and empowered most
Unaware, even with those long tapped roots which could hit the water tables
Not long enough you will be able to entertain us with your formidable talent
Grievances upon who will provide sweeter and juicy fruits to quench our thirst
Our gratitude is incomparable to your words sedimentally laid in black on white
Such a tree which bloomed flamboyantly even off season it was worth a gaze
Healing rain we call upon those which you have invested the seeds in mate
In your caps, you brewed the wine and you kept all the ingredients

Really we are motivated and will continue from where you left
Indeed you proved to us that the world is in need of our unique talent
Probably your pen will lead us to draw conclusions on how to increase the heat.

WHO AM I???
Sheila Banda

I am Strength
An empire I carry
Colossal Hercules has no tale to tell
Being just but an old wives tale
An obsession cum hallucination
Never outstanding the intriguing me.

I am perseverance
Diligence my drive
Faith my stepping stone
Tears my release
Love my habitat
Goodwill my conscience
Victory my sole journey
Courage my moulding pot
& justice my soul's quest.

In silence, a thousand words whisper
Filling the void of what's left unsaid

In silence, a million thoughts unfold
Thoughts of rebuilding abandoned ruins

In silence, troubled waters are calmed
Calmed to pave a safe passage for this adventurous voyager

In silence, a city stands
A city fortified with triumph and splendour

Standing, I do not fall

Determination urges me forward
Forward to achieve the highest mark
An aspiration the heart longs for.

Weary, I do not faint
For I am the beacon others should follow

Scorned, I do not retreat
Defying the cocoon suffocating my dreams.
Instead I bloom,
Bright enough for those inescapable stares
Stares that bore into my very soul
And resuscitate my dormant spirit.

Instead, I shine
With a brightness shadowing all uncertainty
Unleashing unimaginable joy
And bringing immeasurable peace to the being within me.

Cumbersome and stifling it is to be a 'woman'
But being Woman is refreshing and rewarding
For it stands to defy the odds
So I say, I am WOMAN.

CAN'T CROSS BURNT BRIDGES
Sheila Banda

Bitter words are acidic
Bitter words leave a foul aftertaste
Bitter words burn bridges
Bridges already quivering and wobbly from the weight of past scuffles
Bridges overladen with animosity,
They cave in and
Their demise leaves a wedge seemingly difficult to mend
A wedge deep and wide heightened as the years go by.

Smoke of resentment hangs about in the atmosphere
Like a gigantic sullen black cloud pregnant with overdue rain
Roaring thunder is audible; whips of lightning visible
Rather than waiting for destructive, cold, stone sized hail to pelt you
And find yourself surrounded by cinders'
All lonely and soaked, with no companionship and no sanctuary,
Try to mend those bridges for
You can't cross burnt bridges.

Apologise when wrong
Forgive where damage is done
Exchange pride for humility
Trade hatred for love
Flee anger for wisdom
Appreciate where others complain
Give more where it's being withheld from you.

Bite your tongue, once out, bitter words habitat in the minds' archives
They are shelved for time immemorial
They ensnare us
Instead, undo what can be undone

And set the pace for everlasting peace.

To an absent father
Tapuwa Mwedzi

Where were you,
    When I ate dreams for supper
And drank sorrows to quench my thirst,
    When I drove bricks for toys
And soaked the cold into my bones
On mean winter nights,
You were not there and you are not here either.

When I sang praises to other totems
    And received the 'no name, totemless child' tag
You were not there,
So I followed the moon and the stars every night
With the sack of questions slinging on my back

What life could a bastard live?
With 'chants of bad' sang by society's holies
And prophecies of fate ranting on their tongues
I squeezed love,
From the dry teat of my mother's breast,
And passed needle and thread for her
To sew our torn hearts and nurture our solemn dreams
    And she was a mother,
And me-proud to be her 'dirty baby boy'
After finding soap and detergent
To clean up the mess.

Munhandare yeupenyu
Tapuwa Mwedzi

Makanditi ndiri chikei chisina mazino
Vamwe vakati ndiri nhava yakazara mbovo
Vamwewo ndivo vakati ndiri gejo risina mutsago
Vakasandipa mukana wekurimawo rangu gombo reupenyu
Nharaunda yese yakandimomotera senhunzi payemwana tsvina
Zvavaida kundizora hupenzi semadhaka nekusingaperi
Asi mandiri kerunako kamoto kehunhu
Kakaramba kachipfungaira sevhunze remushakata

Ndakaregerera avo vakanditi ndirimbwa ini ndisikahukuri
Vakanditi sekitsi ndinoitira tsvina muhupfu
Seonde ndakaora mukati,
Ndikakumbira kuna musiki mukana munhandare yeupenyu
Ndinongodzana-dzana vadikani
Tarenda richindikwanisa-kwanisa mutimu dzepamberi
Zvibodzwa pano nepapo ndinogohwesa vachiombera
Vanosapota yekwedu timu
NaTafy achiukira vake baba.

An Interview with Philani A. Nyoni
Jabulani Mzinyathi

Zimbolicious welcomes you to this interview. You are an accomplished writer/poet. That is no secret. The essence of this interview is to inspire upcoming poets/writers in general.

JM: Tell us a bit about yourself, areas of interest other than writing. Hopes, dreams, fears if any

PAN: I'm afraid I'll say too much and kill the mystique. Half my readers want to murder me in distinctly elaborate ways; I can't afford to have them think I'm a half-decent human being who scrubs his teeth twice a week.

JM: To what extent is your writing influenced by your background, if at all it is

PAN: I finished school in a dark period in Zimbabwe. We didn't have internet back then, I had no reasonable prospect of attaining tertiary education so all I had were books, mostly the old English masters so for a long time I laughed at free verse. I still think its liberalism is the wobbly backbone supporting most of naked strings of ideas barely coherent to the sensibility masquerading as poetry. That only half defines my literary conscience.

I've wanted to write since I was ten, I'm told I was rhyming before crèche; I suppose that propensity to musicality makes it easy for me to put out 'loud sounding nothings' in the words of Mattenich on the Versailles Treaty. When I write from within I put out half-decent things. And looking back there are crossroads in my life that stand out as defining points in my career; like the time between the ages of eight and ten when I couldn't speak much. Or when I was fifteen and Emmanuel Mpofu, my history teacher, discovered the Master Copy for all the literary pornography I was feeding pubescent peers and invited me to a treaty-conference which ended with me conceding that my works were more noxious than I had previously assumed. And thus began my tutelage in Walter Rodney, Ngugi et al. That's when I started understanding the traditional role of the African Writer. As I grew in wisdom and stature I began to see the world, I saw hopelessness and somehow refused to let it swallow me. If I can transmute the pain to poetry, or any other form of literature or art, then it would have been worth something.

JM: What genre do you like the most? Why are you particularly drawn towards it?

PAN: I love poetry because I appreciate how hard it is to write; I'd rather argue with fourteen lines than forty thousand words. Strangely I picked up the genre later, well after I had started dabbling. I have though been straddling genres recently, as if my spoken-word isn't dramatic enough I've embarked on a quest to turn poetry into film and stage plays. It worked with 'Jane The Ghost', 'Diary of Madness' and the most daring recent wild-child 'The Passions of Black Jesus' which has only staged at the Harare International Theatre Festival and is yet undergoing heavy modifications.

JM: You are a poet. What type of poetry do you write? Why do you choose that style or those styles?

PAN: I write all sorts of poetry. The best description for it is 'experimental'. My sonnets are loosely confined to the tradition: I love half-rhymes, internal rhymes, sometimes I sonnet with anagrams and it makes me feel good inside. Sometimes I am pissed off and just want to rant, so I write whatever I feel. And I wish I could stop feeling things to write in the middle of the night; but then my deepest joy would vanish.

JM: Which poets or writers have influenced your writing in general? Why are you drawn towards those writers?

PAN: There have been a few over the years, and I think every period has its hero. I learn something from every poet I encounter, because Picasso said great artists steal and I believe him because he was a great artist. Not least because he stole!

JM: Tell us about your published works

PAN: My first title was 'Once A Lover Always A Fool', that was published in 2012. Two years later John Eppel and I did 'Hewn From Rock', I followed it up with 'Mars His Sword' in April 2016, that one holds a World Record, a Special Mention (whatever the fuck that is) from the National Arts Merit Awards and a Bulawayo Arts Award for Outstanding Literary Work. I was done with writing then, publishing at least; until Robert Mugabe was deposed and I felt I had to return to active duty. I put out 'Philtrum' one week after his 'resignation' (if you enjoy euphemisms) and updated it after the current president's inauguration. I'm still to be impressed by any other book on the subject, but then I'm biased. By the time this interview is in print I might have a new one in Sweden.

JM: Are you into self-publishing? What are the advantages and disadvantages if any?
PAN: Yes I am. Ironically it's because of my appreciation of traditional publishing. But it's a tonne of work, I only do it because I started writing at a time when Amabooks was the only publisher of poetry worth mentioning in the country. If I hadn't done that then no one would have put out my works. The state of the industry necessitates self-publishing, but one has to be very wary and conscious of what a publisher really does in order to duplicate the process efficiently. And maybe one-up the traditional publisher. I'm pleased to have developed my skills in the craft such that I moonlight for some publishers in things like typesetting, proofreading and editing. But it isn't a walk in the park. If an entire team can take up to nine months to work on a manuscript after the author has decided it's done, why would that same author shortchange us with putting it out two weeks after writing the last word? I for one consistently write just about every day, yet have at least two years between publications. I want to be sure. That's the biggest danger with self-publishing: quality control. I have worked with amazing local and international publishers enough to appreciate them. It's not just about copy editing, writers fall in love with lines, some of them are impotent or unnecessary, some are just overly dressed loud-sounding nothings. Writing is emotional, it's like parenting: nobody wants to be told their child is ugly and needs a plastic surgeon; yet too often necessary.

JM: Upcoming writers/poets usually have this perception that there is a clique of writers that have made it that shut them out. What is your take on that thinking?

PAN: It's absolutely true. There is a clique of people who have mutual respect for each other because they have seen war and understand the necessities of getting the job done. They admire each other for what they have endured, sometimes together, to gain their stature and arrange those woods/words so painstakingly. They meet often in the same spaces and ask things of each other that the asked is scared to say no to because of what Paulo Coelho calls 'the favour bank'. The bank and the mutual admiration bordering on fetishism is what makes it easier for them to do things for each other. It's nothing personal, but that's what makes it hard for someone who does not speak the language to gain any traction with this illuminati. When we all come into the industry we all have illusions. Sometimes these writers who seem to have made it share a common disillusionment, sometimes they share a common illusion.

I found the perfect metaphor for life in this journey while hiking in the mountains of Mozambique with a good friend Jenna recently: When you're at the bottom it looks like the top is fifty metres up; then you climb higher and at a hundred and twenty metres you find some people who were so ahead of you, you think the mist on the top is their cooking-fire. So you stand there with them, some are fed up with the climb and will make camp there, some want to go back down already, some are already climbing and won't listen to you, but most of you just hang around together, looking up, discussing which is the best side to scale it from.

JM: How many books have you published to date?

PAN: Three and a half. The half was with John Eppel. All my solo works had been award-winning until 'Philtrum' and its explosive subject-matter. That might seem disappointing until it gets into the hands of a Swedish publisher who decides to put out a new collection of translated works for the Swedish market. So that will be five by the end of the year; I will probably spend a while trying to pronounce the title of my fifth.

JM: Which one is your favourite? Why is that so?

PAN: No parent should ever be made to choose which of his children he loves best; but at gunpoint I would say 'Once A Lover Always A Fool'. Your first project is the longest and most meticulous one. In my most private moments, I concede that I'll never write something as complete. Maybe I have, but I like to think that.

JM: Have you won awards if so tell us which ones?

PAN: A few. I'm the first and only Zimbabwean poet to be awarded National Arts Merit Awards for Literature and Spoken Word. I received my first one for 'Once A Lover Always A Fool' at twenty-three, three years later I earned the Spoken Word one. That's also the same year 'Jane The Ghost', a film I co-wrote and shot won 'Outstanding Short-film'. 'Mars His Sword' received a Bulawayo Arts Award in 2017, the same year it got 'special mention' at the National Arts Merit Awards. My short story 'Celestial Incest' was shortlisted for the African Writers' Award in 2018. Before all that I received a First Class nod at the Girls' College Literary in 2016 'Honours', the following year along with the 'Best Poem' award for a piece titled 'Shakespeare'. 'Mars His Sword' also set the World Record for 'Most Shakespearean Sonnets in a Manuscript'. It was officially verified by Record Setter and still stands. I wrote 308 at 26, Shakespeare died at twice that age, his official collection has half of that.

JM: Are your works raking in a lot of financial rewards?

PAN: So the taxman sent you this time? Et tu Brute? Next question.

JM: What inspires you to write poetry/ prose?

PAN: The shortest answer is 'anything'. The nature of inspiration has been debated for years, but I like the German attitude towards it: it's possession, the demon is very rude and knocks at strange moments.

JM: What do you think of the state of writing in Zimbabwe currently?

PAN: This is an entire dissertation on its own.

JM: This country is reeling under an economic tsunami, to what extent has this influenced your writing?

PAN: In 2014 Noviolet Bulawayo recommended me to The Caine Prize for African Writing and I spent two weeks crafting a story with some of the hardest fiction writers of my time. Most of them were out there, published by real publishers, international, well-traveled and with fierce reputations. I was just that strange kid from Zimbabwe. My hair was wild, I wore this tracksuit and white t-shirt that should have been relegated to a skorobho a long time ago. I was the youngest among them and probably the least known. I remember how blown away they were the first time I read my project. I also remember how they drove me to drink spirits (I had been on beer the whole time) the second time they heard me read. One would ask if I wasn't propping up the stereotype of 'poverty-porn' by undressing the regime, I was cautioned by someone who used a pseudonym because they were very-very close to the First Family: they didn't have illusions about what those in power do to people like me. I had been counselled not to 'sell the country' before I went to that workshop but I did. I thought about my situation, what I would go back to when the four-star luxury of those two weeks was over. I lived in a tiny room, slept on the floor, hardly ate for two days within a week of leaving that workshop; I assure you, I had no regrets for writing what I had left on those pages now published as 'The Soneeteer'. I remember my response to the sell-out question, right in front of a crackling fire, drink in hand and barman ever poised to serve whatever poison the spirit hungered: 'if you had one chance to tell a story, and you knew it was going to be published anyway, in ten countries; wouldn't you tell the most important story you had inside you?' The story was that some will never be great or appreciated for their gifts and energy as much as they should be because we are here, now. But while I have this opportunity, I'll punch as hard as I can. Memory Chirere called it 'the craziest story in the book' when he reviewed the collection; it was only a portrait of the times.

JM: There are lots of upcoming poets/writers out there. What advice would you give them so that they really hit some measure of success?

PAN: Just write. Read. And write. And read.

JM: Briefly tell us what writing endeavours you are currently engaged in
PAN: I'm always threatening to retire. I had succeeded until the November coup. Right now I feel like John Wick: all I wanted to do was kill the guy who murdered my dog, now I'm tearing through a bunch of bad guys with half the stamina that made my name. I hope 'The Passions of Black Jesus will be my last effort, if not then look out for something called 'Virgin Blood & Lingerie'.

JM: Please, please, please share with us three, of any of your poems

Poems by Philani A Nyoni:

How I Became Spartacus

The crosshairs of fate saw me stark in the street
Amidst a flurry of anger and violence.
I stopped to watch the inferno that had been lit
On the corner of Tenth and Fort, after I'd wept;
Not for the pain in my soul nor the rags
My home has become: brothers devolved to beast
Straining the constrain of a shit-stained flag,
Not for my dreams (not iron) that had been creased
And tossed into the bin alongside my savings,
Their pensions -there is none for what I do-
But the indiscriminate force of police and teargas.
I hid in the library when I was done braving
The assault, walked home ere the sky changed hue.
I should have slept in the next day but the crass
Air called me outside to inhale a country burning.
You should know, as I type this, I'm waiting
For the police to kick down my door and set fire
To my nuts with some electric contraption of torture.
In all this what is my crime? I too wish, nay, aspire
For a new country to be born, but this is my occupation,
I have no employer to raise hell against... or expectation,
And I'm too famous to do crazy shit on the street.
I waved at but did not take part in the demonstration,
What I do is more personal, and more discreet.
So you can imagine my consternation, dear reader,
When I found my name in the pages of The Guardian*.
They were right, I think we have suffered enough,
I think the policies of the government are stupid,
But I think the price hike is justified, the dildo currency

Is broken and not trading well beyond our borders.
But I try to keep my opinion of the currency or the men
At the helm out of the media, just in poems and stuff.
But the government has blocked the communication grid
So I can't denounce the devil with the urgency
It demands. So now, I only await the soldiers orders,
Wondering, if the journalists in white countries are like ours
Who make up quotes to spice up their letters.
Surely there are enough corpses to speak the horror.
Maybe some silly fuck protest-brave but shy for the camera
Gave a statement and wrapped it in my name.
Today I have a dangerous name, like Spartacus.
Now I'm not sure if I still want to be famous
(Hearing this my Christian tattoos choired:
To whom much is given much shall be required)
It could also be an elaborate plan to get me killed.
I have a great dilemma my friend, but all the same,
Fuck it, let them come and bury the knife to the hilt,
They can hang me for treason, right next to Corday,
Or put a bullet in my msundulo and... I don't know, say
I evaded arrest and tried to run away from the police gang.
Isn't that what we all want? To go out with a bang?

*We have suffered enough,' said Philani Nyoni, an author who was part of the protest in Bulawayo. The government is now aware that we are not happy with their stupid policies like the fuel price increase.' -The Guardian, 14 January 2019

Chimanimani

Some come here to live in tents;
Not these, caught between god and man.
The high wrath that sawed, mountains rent,
Washed them here, to pray in vain
To the kindness of meddlers not long in office
But answered by kindred, slightly less hopeless
While elected seats fly sofas in choppers
Over homes, wives, goats and children
Drowning, floating, to the Indian Ocean.
And the sofas have flown away,
Will they return? Who can say?
When the wives, the children and goats
Decide to float back home?
And now there are only tents to stay,
Not like the tourists', these might be here
Until the rain returns. And beyond.

Nadir

Sometimes I shout so you can hear me.
Between our silences there's a crackling;
My soul in the petals of my yoke; can't you hear?
Not while you're trembling in your pain.
We said love would conquer fear.
Now our love is aching.
I reach for your face, it's all in vain,
Night and timezones won't let us be;
So I scream because you are far
And winter's rattling on my scars
And I should remind you to die only once;
To carry those who go before you,
Don't follow them into the ground.
But you can't hear me like it's not aloud
And I'm scared of what I'm about to do:
Cut you deep so you spare me a glance
If my worth hasn't faded after our dance,
Wasn't just a boy you needed to feel young:
A drought of skunk to shake your lung.
I'm screaming! hoping you hear me
As if your sadness could ever cheer me.

"The Word is gibberish, the plot Absurd."

-Derek Walcott

JM: Lastly Zimbolicous thanks you for taking time to participate in this interview. All the best in all you do.

Fiction

The unknown b
Mushumbi Aaron F

He thinks, they will be never enough time to read. This thought asphyxiate him. Aaron. A gentleman in his late thirties. He suffers from myopia and utopia. His world is only the books he reads through the night. Endlessly and everyday and he is insatiable. An avid reader. He has lost contact with reality. The books are his reality and the reality his books. A hopeless situation. He shivers – craving – for books. Premature greying hair on his head. Short not well groomed hair. He does not drink strong beverages. Neither does he smoke crack. Nor knowledge of the birth canal. Aaron thinks himself levitical. Perpetual vows on poverty – will explain – vows on chastity, also an explanandum.

To the right and left of his studying desk there are photogenic pictures of beautiful girls. Women. There is a difference in meaning between girls and women. Girls are full of sugar, but can't resist that women are also full of sugar. One picture, a dark, perfect giant. In navy jeans, tight on her and a dubious smile. Pensively staring at the camera lenses before the shatter goes off. Aaron has non to it. Its philosophy. Axiology. Too good a case study of mermaids and copulation. Appetising. His father a canonist and are friends and alike. His father superstitions of witches that bewitched gran gran. His philial milipeding or dried caterpillar especially in freezing weather. She is expensive in outlook and Aaron dares not describe the inlook. Colours dangerously beautiful. Detoured colours and in descript. One can just say good. His mother high pitched in voice. Explanans.

Finding the missing number. Aaron is a primary school teacher – who learnt pedagogies in the dog days of political consciousness. Kind of congregats refusing to paean any more. Same age – but he was thrown in the gallows for a decade and came back detached from the world – nostalgia thinking 2019 is 1998 and can't move from there. A mental incurable disease and though weaned his mother takes care of him on that aspect or he will think he is still six. He doesn't know that. Two; four; b and eight. Six makes sense. For juveniles with a democratic teacher like Syllabus A prescribes as the best. And it's permissible. Bread and butter for the poor. Teachers, nurses, police.

Two; ten; twenty five; fifty escalating and sky rocketing. An egg. Homeward. Five hundred; five hundred and one. They like that topic. Numbers. And one of the objectives is to say, write and read numbers in words and digits. And Aaron gives them endless notes. Descriptive and not defunct. The kind of thinking in its simplest, original and best form is the brain child of Margret Artwood – *The Blind Assassin*. And Aaron was reading, *Agent in Place* by Helen – she is good again, but gained that he will not venture into politics or spy business or any form of intelligence and diplomacy. Dirty. He loves his life. Very. Shelves and shelves of books. Thick copies. And Mandela dug his own grave in *No Easy Walk to Freedom*. Aaron is departing for Harare on Saturday, seething for Daniele Steele. These girls are the definition of seduction and Marechera fucked his female character in a story he was writing. Mad.

They understand. Pa was true. And Ma. Aaron discovered the definition of Kleptomania and it placed him right on track US$ 50 on 100 rtgs its everything and she was smiling ruby red lips. Dark pupilled eyes. A doll. Aaron playing chess and castling and piercing bewildered shouts – from nowhere and shivering and an erection, bad combination and eureka. Plays no more, where the hell *Black Sunlight* at 100 pounds. The smile was good, but she refused to kiss him. Is that what you want, it will be censored. There and then.

He likes his mother because her marginal propensity to consume is very low and good. And her marginal propensity to save is good. Basics. That is mealie gruel. He has a strong appetite for meat. And leadership is intelligent. He is reading philosophy and will go to law. *The Communist Manifesto*, introduction to politics. He does not know – what they say about cold blooded murderer – but he read briefly culpable homicide and soft skull theory. Philosophy, that is of science say theology is meaningless and poetry and literature and he agrees. I want to give people bread and flowers. Let me sleep. The theory of Thomas Kahn or maybe falsiability – if the road leads to

Mbare, home of Povo, then you are a hero. He doesn't have any original opinion on that as is the explanation I have promised.

The girl or the woman as we have agreed says, his opinions are not fine and researched. Complete strangers, but next of skin when the weather is fine. Too bookish. But detastes anarchism, maybe intellectual. The other picture well photoshopped depicting a pleasant girl in white not very tights. He asked her if she played him, but could not get to the bottom of the story. She didn't smile. Massive another definition of the unknown b.

    20/06/2019   2035 mutukwana no electricity

Seven
Matthew K Chikono

Last Friday evening I came back from work and found Flora cooking supper. A tantalising smell of beef stew struck my nose as I entered the kitchen and there she was, in her pink satin dress looking a decade younger and more beautiful than ever. Stirring the sadza in the favorite black pot, she smiled and told me that dinner would be ready in a few minutes. Before she could order me out of the kitchen, I went out to clean up before dinner was served. When I came back, I found her in front of the black oven, taking out those hot lemon scones I like very much. I won't lie, it was the best meal I have ever had in a very long time. Flora had been dead for seven months.

"Seven years," Chamunorwa always whispers in my ear, "Flora has been dead for seven years Gilbert."

He is my friend and he loves me. I am sure he does, I mean how can he be my best friend for seventy years and not get crazy. It must be seventy years including those years our mothers were pregnant teenagers. My earliest memory of us is that of us both dressed in napkins made of old torn shirts, pooping together in my mother's kitchen. We might have been two or three years old. Alas, there were no cameras, to preserve these rare memories.

He is old, so am I, but he looks the youngest among the trio of us. An old greyish wool hat sits on his head, donning a peculiar smile on his naked gums and a huge waistcoat I gave him on his third wedding seventeen years ago. Chamunorwa always gulps down some millet beer he thinks or says anything worth your time. He believes that the masese is the real and only poison that had kept him alive all these years. I like him, I have to like him or else I will be friendless for the remainder of my days which unfortunately are not much now.

"Seven years," Chamunorwa whispers in my ear, "Flora has been dead for seven years Gilbert."

We are sitting outside Zvidozvevanhu beerhall on a Sunday evening. At least it's a cool day, I am always cold these days and I hate it. The people of Chitungwiza are rushing to the vegetable stalls to buy the fresh ingredients of their supper in the process raising unnecessary dust. It hasn't rained in a while and we are choking with the dust but what else can we do, we are old men with nothing else to do.

"Seven years," Chamunorwa whispers in my again in my left ear, "Flora has been late for seven years my dearest friend."

There is no need to whisper the beerhall is empty, it's always empty. Young people don't drink here, they never will. They prefer night clubs or the new fancy sports bar next door were modern music is played too loud.

They don't play loud music in Zvidozvevanhu beerhall nor do they play music at all. This beerhall is old, we have been drinking here since we were teenagers. I like it nothing ever changes in here. It's always empty and quiet and I always tell Chamunorwa not to whisper but he always does, old habits never die at all.

"Yes, seven years," I mutter with embarrassment, "My wife has been dead for seven years."

I cannot bear to think what they are thinking of me; a man who doesn't remember how long his wife has been late. I might not remember how long it was but I know all the pain I went through. She didn't die peacefully in her bed while I sat beside her holding her hand, no. She was electrocuted to death.

The old power lines ran underneath our backyard and one stormy afternoon, Flora walked barefooted on top of an exposed wire. I was watching her walk away from me, I hated it but she always made it beautiful. She never screamed. Her body was thrown few metres away. I saw smoke coming out from every part of her before the smell of burning flesh hit my nose. I raced to save my wife. I ran to my beloved Flora and there was nothing else to be done except cover her body and weep. She was 62.

"Yes, seven years," I mutter with embarrassment, "My wife has been dead for seven years."

Not that I am proud but I have to say I am the smartest and the most intelligent of my friends and it is unheard of me to forget anything. I cannot even blame alcohol, I have never taken it in my life. It is definitely strange that I would forget that it has been seven years since I saw Flora die. In Zimbabwe load shedding is up to 18 hours a day and on average less than five people die because of electrical shocks. To the world Flora is now just part of statistics, a mere number that saves no purpose to those who loved her. It is a terrible way to die and a horrible way to lose your soulmate.

"Yes, seven years sure," I mutter with shame and embarrassment, "My wife has been late for seven years and it's unbelievable that I forgot the day my wife of fifty years passed away."

We meet at Nyadire teacher's college where we were both students in the late 50s.

"My name is Flora, just like Roman goddess of flowers." That was the first thing she said as she sat down next to me in the school library and I was in love. I have told this story a million times before that I am starting to believe it's true. It's not. Everyone thinks it's the best love story ever told, even Flora thought it sweet for the rest of her life. I can't say I lied, I only simplified the story.

She was in her first year and I was in my third and final year of our teaching diplomas when I first noticed her in the library. She was a bookworm and I was just an avid reader who wanted to read half of the books in the library. She always sat on the chair next to Shona fiction section. Honestly all the books I had read weren't of any help on how I could talk to her. I did the only other thing that I thought was romantic, I sat on her chair one day.

"You are sitting on my chair."

"I am sorry?" I pretended to be surprised, "This chair and everything that is within this library belongs to the school, are you aware of that?"

I could see it in her eyes that she knew but she didn't care, all she wanted was the perfect reading spot.

"You are Flora, right?" I asked with a false dawn of recognition on my face, "Flora like the Roman goddess of flowers."

She wore a white blouse and a toe length coloured skirt that day. Sockless she wore a semi-heeled black shoe. Her hair was cut short and huge specs covered her eyes. She was just an angel that had recently lost its wings.

"I sit here every day reading and you can pack your things and leave, it will make things easier for everyone."

"Yes Chloris!" I continued with our deep philosophical chat, "Chloris is her Greek counterpart, by the way will you marry me?"

"Yes!" she gladly answered six years later after I had asked for the dozenth time. We got married and lived happily ever after.

"So, you are saying your wife came back from the dead and is now cooking delicious food for you?" Chamunorwa asks as an afterthought, his attention more focused on the beer than the question.

"No, he said his dead wife is alive," says our other companion whom I think is crazy, "I think he is crazy."

Tichafara is not our friend but he is always there for us for a very long time. We got acquainted when he first decided to spend his Sundays drinking beer at our bar than spend it at a local baptist church where he was a pastor.

"My wife came back to me," I calmly say, "she is well and alive."

"Mwariwe!" Chamunorwa chokes in disbelief, "Don't tell me you visited Sekuru Ngara?"

"Sekuru Ngara the witch?"

"No, Sekuru Ngara the healer."

"Same thing." Tichafara says spitting, "that old man is no good."

He spits again. Tichafara hates Sekuru Ngara that's not a secret. A physical fight between the two had resulted in Tichafara losing his job as a pastor. No one knows what the argument was all about.

"Tell me Gilbert," Chamunorwa says removing his hat, "what did that man give you?"

"Or worse, what did he do to you?"

"Nothing," I say to them with my magic smile, "he just told me to go home."

From the way they are looking at me I can tell they don't believe me, they will never do.

"Fine," I sigh, "he told me to bath in the Nyatsime River at midnight for seven nights."

"In this kind of weather?"

"Bathing in the cold river was the act necessary to test your dedication and commitment. It was an act of faith and you passed. Now tell us, what did you pay for it?" Tichafara says thoughtfully. He is clever and I really thank God that Tichafara doesn't believe in God anymore, how else would I learn this deep philosophical stuff from this man? I honestly believe that his efforts would have been wasted on those church people if he had continued preaching at the church, modern christians deserve to go to hell after all.

"Tichafara, Gilbert has just been given some witchcraft or worse, a spiritual wife and we need to help him!"

"Or maybe the little headache hasn't gone away yet dear Chamunorwa."

Oh yes, my little headache. My friends call it a little headache but it's worse, psychosis. I have been diagnosed of it for a while but I am fine, I think I am fine. Flora is back, do I have to care if it's the psychosis or the medicine Sekuru Ngara gave me? No, I am happy. I have everything I desire although it's just for seven days. My friends bewail around me and I sip my mahewu silently, patiently waiting for Flora to come back to me for another seven nights.

STRANGE THINGS HAPPEN
Christopher Kudyahakudadirwe

A wintry wind whistles through the weary willow trees behind us. The cold seems to have been dragging on for far too long than usual this season. A few clouds sail across the blue sky like white water-lily leaves on the surface of a blue pool. Although the temperatures are low the day is bright with the sun being blocked in short episodes by the north-westerly bound clouds. The air smells sterile except for the slight whiff of perfume that drifts from the lady who stands next to me.

For as long as we have been standing here, the lady has not turned to look at me but that does not stop me from looking at her through the corner of my eye. It is not my making that I should be standing here, but my friend and his wife called me to come and be with them as they address the young people gathered here with whom they were to go on an excursion. I am to make my mind as to join them later. A good number of the youths have gathered and are standing in groups of twos and threes on the open ground before us, chatting to one another animatedly about the trip – so I think – as I am not close enough to hear the subject of their bubbling. We are waiting for all the boys and girls to arrive.

"Max," I turn to my friend who is standing between the lady and his wife on the other side.

"What time do you expect everyone to be here?"

"We told them to be here by 10am." He looks at his wrist. "And we still have half an hour before 10."

"Judging by the number already here, it would seem they will all arrive very soon." As if by infection, I also check my watch.

"Yes, and they are also very eager to climb the mountain." Max's wife chimes in.

The lady, whose name I later learnt to be Letwin, seems unbothered by neither the prevailing weather conditions nor the subject of our discourse at this moment. Like a horse with blinkers she kept her round face looking ahead, and I felt the invisible Berlin wall that she seems to maintain between us thickening. Since when have I been shy to look at the faces of ladies? This question keeps popping into my mind every time I take sneaked looks at her. These snuck glances at the young woman reward me with a rich garden of womanhood which has been endowed and nurtured on this human being.

"Max," I am almost sweating under the pressure of wanting to be alone with this lady and telling her about the riot of emotions raging in my mind. "I'll take Letwin to buy coffees at the service station over there. We'll be back soon, soon." I announce that as if I have already agreed with Letwin about going to the shop.

"That's okay. And please bring me a packet of cigarettes." He gives me some money.

Letwin did not disagree with my proposal for a walk away from Max and his wife, so we saunter from the couple like a couple that has been together for some time. She displays a dignified gaiety that is not common among women of her type. Now I can look at her face whose features are as sharp as if they were chiseled out of granite, with dark languid eyes filling their meant positions on her small round face. Small pimples grace her fair skin without much consequence. Her breasts are small lemons punctuating her steps with bounces that would entice anyone seeing them to want to harvest them and make lemonade. Like a winding staircase, I turn to check what is at her back; her rounded bum pronounce her an epitome of God's exquisite creation to its best – they bounce with each step in a way that make me want to forget that I am going forward.

So, with all this having been uploaded into my brain, we walk side by side for a while before none of us has garnered enough courage to speak. As it was my first time to see her, this could be the reason why I have found it difficult to summon much courage to speak to her. She has been presented to me without warning, and I am sure she also has the same foreboding feeling about speaking to me. So far, I have not heard her voice, but my ears are itching to pick the timbre of it.

"Let's get ourselves some coffees from the service station." I break the suffocating silence ultimately, forgetting that I had already announced this before we left where we had been standing with Max and his wife.

"I prefer cappuccino."

I raise my eyebrows. "You have a lovely voice."

She speaks like a cello played in an empty hall; all husky and deep-throated.

"Thank you. Not many people have said that to me." Letwin steals a glance at me for the first time. Her dark eyes sweep over my face like an unintended caress — a soft feather moved by the wind over my skin - as they quickly scan my features. How I wish I had the privilege to peer into their depths to fathom what dwells in them.

As we approach the service station, Letwin excuses herself to go and use the bathroom. I wait for her near the pumps. When she comes back, she has taken off the dress she was wearing and is now wearing a pinkish one. I do not know where she has put the previous one nor where the pinkish one had materialised from; perhaps she was wearing both dresses at one time. I do not say anything about that, but I look askance as to how that had happened, for she did not have a handbag that could fit any garment bigger than a handkerchief.

At the service station, we buy our drinks and the cigarettes for Max.

"May I have your cellular number?" I ask her knowing that when we get back to Max and his wife, I may forget to ask for it. Without hesitation, she takes out a pen from her purse and writes: 071 546 9199 on a page she tears from what looks like a diary. I take the paper and put it in my pocket after looking at for a while. She smiles at me as she replaces her diary-like book into her purse and closes it.

As we walk back to Max, I imagine myself fondling her lemon-sized breasts and as stated before, making lemonade from them, and finally kissing her all over everywhere, but this cannot be done as I imagine because I am carrying the drinks in my hands and secondly, we have barely come to that level of knowing each other as to be allowed such luxuries. When we are about to get to where we left the others, I put down my coffee and go for what I am imagining. Letwin does not resist. Then I see Max coming around the corner and … I wake up. I realised I am only dreaming!

*

I check the time on the wall clock. It is 06:29. I am late for work. I should have been up at 6 o'clock already. Quickly I get into the cold shower as if to extinguish all the fires that have been lit in the dream, throw clothes on and dash to the car to add to the traffic in the morning rush hour. I arrive at work at 08:17. After settling in my office, my mind runs over the details of the dream that I had. It is still so vivid. The face of Letwin is still imprinted in my mind, her softness still lingers in my fingers and her perfume is still wafting into my nose. The dream was so real. One thing that struck me is that the number she had written on that paper in the dream is still stuck in my mind. I immediately enter it in my phone book.

Work is sluggish: filing tax returns for the company, sending out emails to prospective customers and in between, cups and cups of coffee.

At 10, out of curiosity, I decide to call the number that Letwin had given me in the dream.

"Hello." A female voice answers from the other end.

"Hello, Letwin." I am just trying out that name since it belonged to the girl in the dream.

"How did you get my number?"

"You gave it to me … in- in a dream. Are you Letwin?"

"Which dream? That's impossible. You're lying. Who are you?"

"Perhaps." I sit up in the chair. "But that is what happened. I had a dream in which a girl named Letwin gave me her number." I am feeling stupid about the whole thing now. "It was so vivid that I remember the number even now. And for curiosity's sake I decided to dial it."

"Who are you?"

"Kudzi."

"Strange things are happening, if I'm to go by what you're telling me." There is a brief silence on the end of the line. "You must have got my number from someone who knows me. Where are you?"

"I'm in Mutare and you?"

"Chinhoyi."

"I've never been in Chinhoyi. According to my knowledge you could be the first person from there that I'm beginning to know."

My communication with Letwin is still going on. She has sent me pictures of herself and, good God, how she resembles the lady in my dreams! We're going to meet very soon. I've made a strong obligation to go and visit Chinhoyi in order to meet Letwin, this time not in a dream.

NOAH'S ARK

Sheila Banda

After being verbally massacred, his dignity torn into shreds, Farai salvaged his remains with a lump in his throat. He groped for the chair as a blind man does without a backward glance. He had prepared himself to sit but had remained suspended, trying to absorb the shock of it all. His shirt could not hold the strain as it found its way out of the trousers. The pressure being too much, Farai heaved his bulk upon the hard, rickety piece of furniture which creaked for mercy. His misplaced shirt exposed charcoal black occupants epitomising two hot buns buckling under pressure. He felt much heavier as the weight of humiliation was an added load to his gigantic frame. His troubled and disturbed mind kept him fidgeting throughout the remaining minutes of the meeting. His sweat glands suddenly became more porous than before threatening to channel hot boiling blood moving in his veins. Anger, embarrassment, vengeance, bitterness mingled with fear was all bottled up in him.

The silence after this cutting edge episode was threatening. A pin drop could have produced an echo. Tension was so visible and tangible that one could tear off its fabric and produce a jacket out of it just to cover Farai's embarrassment. No one dared move. It was a bad moment frozen in time. Not a single whisper. People fumbled with their fingers, some were trying to remove their freshly painted nail polish. Some succeeded and the evidence was right on their skirts. Men were even straightening their trousers and trying to make them longer. Some were putting their askew ties back in place. Some were staring at their feet as if it was still a wonder to them how they could possess such beautiful things! Everyone was somewhere and busy but there feigning absentmindness . Only the howling wind you could hear. Trees swayed fiercely back and forth. Women's oily drenched wigs were violently torn from their heads exposing kinky unkempt hair. Leaves were strewn all over the congregates. Sand grains were thrown in people's faces but no one dared complain. Women took cover under their "zambias" whilst men shielded themselves with their hands, heads bowed down. Dark grey clouds

116

were looming in the distance threatening to burst any time soon. Animals were scurrying about for cover sensing imminent danger. The weather, the tension, painted a gloomy picture.

All this while, Monica seemed to be perusing her notes. She did it slowly and carefully as if waiting for something to happen for her to stop this monotonous action. It was a diversion from her thoughts. It was a distraction. She had expected an outburst from the mighty, colossal Farai but instead got the shock of her life. Silence. The Surrender, the buckling in was something she did not envisage. Was this a conquest to be celebrated over? Had she tamed the revered and honoured one with her only weapon and ammunition, her words? But this, this episode, this occurrence was an enigma she had to solve. Her nerves were all jittery but she would not for the sake of her pride and a minute long victory ever show it. What have I done? But she knew that when the elephants fight, the grass bear the brunt. She was going to be in this for the long haul and this was just the welcoming remarks. For now, she was in possession of the last laugh and she wondered how many last laughs she was going to pocket.

"Ahem", Monica cleared her throat, "I will handover to Mr Chairman to finalise the proceedings of this meeting. Mr Chigariro over to you." The short stout man leapt into action and took his Chairman's position. He bellowed into the microphone and his booming voice caught people off guard and shook them into reality.

"This meeting is adjourned", he said, "and we will advise of another meeting pending the results of the findings from our discussions. Minutes will be availed on a date still to be announced. Thank you for your contributions, concerns and for the time you invested in attending. Thank you for the unity of purpose for 'united we stand and divided we fall'. The war for development and transparency still continues 'aluta continua'. May you go in peace and stay in peace. Thank you!"

Responding to this dismissal, nursing mothers raptured their breasts from their suckling babes who howled in demonstration. Some were ridding themselves of dust accumulated courtesy of the windy weather. Everyone was hastening, men already quickening their pace for a heavy downpour was eminent. It was a long walk back to the village and only those in possession of vehicles were lingering about.

Farai was robbed of a dignified exit. He was left with a tail between his legs. His elite group feigned not to notice. Mr Chigariro was the first to approach him exchanging pleasantries and sharing tit bits about family life. People were mingling and such occasions stretched to unnecessary ridiculous long hours. Some would be weighing each other's progress and success and boasting about their achievements. Those waiting for free rides from their privileged counterparts were standing in their own group. These were typical wannabes who yearned to be associated with success although it was a long way from them. They had to endure the biting weather whilst discussing noneties and pretended not to be moved by the previous events.

Far out in the road, a cloud of dust trailed behind people hurrying to their respective homes. They were conversing along the way. You could hear cackles of laughter and clapping of palms in joy.

The once sombre gathering came into life. One gossip mongers, Mai Runyararo, voice was aloof,

"Askana today's events heeeei, God is there", clicking her fingers for emphasis, "Farai being cut down to size like that. God is for everyone and God is not a stupid!" Awhile, her plump hands resting on her heaving, bulging chest, she saw Gods goodness and vengeance in people's embarrassments, which was her inbuilt mechanism, a sadist in the making. No one in her presence would utter a sentence to support her for one day it would haunt you. Instead you could hear women chorusing 'yes, yes it's true' in response. Men were basing about in their baritones

"Surely each dog has its day. Mmmm Monica saying that to Farai amidst all of us, she is stepping on something surely. Something is brewing or has already been brewed. This should be written in the genus book of records I tell you." Baba Chikwavairo marvelled.

"I saw it from the first that Farai was no match for Monica. I said it and people thought I was just a jealous hare in the book only moved by the turning of pages! Hehehehe! Today my prophecy has been fulfilled."

"Iwee Samson, this time around you were right. They say what goes around comes around."

Such conversations were doing the rounds and people couldn't wait to relay the proceedings to those at home, those perturbed by the unfriendly weather. It began to drizzle and an appetising scent of wet soil rose into the atmosphere. The tempo increased. The heavily saturated clouds unleashed their anger on mother earth in great torrents. There was no place to scurry for cover for people had covered a distance. Umbrellas were raised in a bid to shield themselves from the downpour. Thunder rumbled, lightning cracked and the wind whipped away umbrellas and plastics held by feeble fingers.

Trees swayed and bent back and forth as if they would snap. Rain plummeted bare haired heads with such vigour as if it was a punishment for an unknown offence. Ladies held hands in unison for fear of being carried away in the maddening weather. You could hear 'maiwees' and cursing from people. They were drenched and soaked to the bone and the heavy downpour reduced their momentum and they were wadding about like ducks in the muddy terrain. Mother nature was in a rage and if this was an omen of things to come, at least they had seen better days.

Sekuru Chogugudza trailed far behind the chattering, excited and drenched people, his bent figure supported by his roughly craven walking stick. One could fear that his hands would be ripped off by the rough edges of the stick. No meeting would pass without his attendance nomatter how far the distance. The energy he possessed didn't equal his old age thus prompting villagers to align him to wizardly's powers. Word was his walking stick was actually an ominous python which sapped strength from villagers as they slept. His neighbour, though lazy in nature, concocted stories of how he saw the python draining blood from his deceased wife whilst Sekuru was standing straight and his face looking youthful with teeth full in his mouth grinning and urging on his 'lover', the python. This, he says happened a night before his wife passed on. But everyone knew how Mharapara loved chasing skirts as he liked chasing stories and brought the disease upon himself.

Sekuru had been a teacher once with ZJC a qualification and was not accustomed to have stale news brought to him. He was an informed and alert old man who had surpassed his former colleagues' life expectancy because of his wise ways. His grandchildren adored him and his children worshipped

119

him. He retained most of his old ways and refused to embrace some modern ways his children wanted to enforce in him. His notion was that modernisation had driven young people into an early grave. The food which encouraged obesity and diseases associated with it, televisions which he labelled the devil incarnate as they spread immorality etc etc. He said back then in his time, girls used to be real girls and men used to be real men but nowadays the whole lot was like a bunch of crumpled and creasy second hand clothes from Mupedzanhamo (second hand clothes mall)!

"Tsk, tsk", he would click his tongue, "what an obscene generation."

As he trudged along in the downpour embracing God's gift upon earth and taking in every drop, he was mumbling to himself. In all the excitement and drama, no one offered a word of prayer to end the meeting. He marvelled at how this generation labelled themselves Christians and mocked the traditional ways. Suddenly a car pulled over just near sekuru. As the driver rolled down his window he recognised his great grandson, Tumai.

"Old boy come on in." with a loving smile plastered on his face. Sekuru walked gracefully to the opened door and took his seat.

"Life has been kind to you sekuru but you not as young as you used to be or want to be. Why walk all the way to the meeting and endanger yourself in this bloody weather?"

Every drop of water he had soaked was now dripping on the seat and forming a pool on the floor. He sneezed here and there for the warmth of his environment and his dampness was two opposing factors. Sekuru took his time before responding as was his character.

"Farai was ridiculed by Monica, his girlfriend because she is now his boss's mistress. Eey this life! A life of lost causes."

With that sekuru sealed his lips and sneezed violently as his body jerked forward in unison to the roaring thunder and whip of lightning. The car shook vigorously and Tumai applied brakes. He looked at his sekuru and couldn't help wonder how these signs exhibiting his approval or discontentment over something followed him. It was true what they said that with age comes wisdom, applied to though with some only wrinkles come with age.

"So what should be done sekuru to restore dignity to this life then?" Tumai asked

"Mwana wemuzukuru wangu, zvakaoma. (My great grandson, its mind boggling) We need Noah's ark."

"What? Noah's ar…. Why Sekuru?" Tumai couldn't finish his sentence coz he was perplexed at this unexpected response.

"That's what we need Tumi, that's the only solution." With that Sekuru rested his case and Tumai started the car and they travelled in silence until they reached their destination.

VISUAL ART

Exams and Blooming Jacarandas (November 2014)
Victor Gordon Musara

Glory be to you Christ for these
blooming Jacarandas
with ramified leafless branches
pointing at the clear welkin of
this Savannah noon
with their delicate purple

flowers scattered all over the
school courtyard.
they stir my memory of a time
at this same place
the days when i was still little
and had to cross a stream much
ordinary
than this brine before me.

Thank you Lord for this invisible
air
whose existence is a mystery,
yon' what my mind can fathom,
yet its presence remains tangible
as long as my heart beats
even at a rate lower than this:
the beat from the choir
percussion
and adrenaline much lower.

the caprices of my heart
with a faith so feeble
distance me from You.
have mercy on me O' Christ
and carry me across this brine
lest these days become a vivid
poignant memory
haunting me
till death.

rains (2017)
Victor Gordon Musara

A cloak of black mist adorns our Vale;
black clouds cap scarred mountains:
A tentative promise of rains,

fertility, and a good harvest.

Filled with hope,
we till the land,
we toil.
But our lilies shrivel in the rain.
Did the heavens make an empty promise?

Beneath the mines,
rather, beneath what's left of the mountains,
the earth rumbles and crumbles
at the hands of men ferreting for gems
which are flown to foreign lands.
In the mayhem, black fumes rise to the skies
to court the crisp clouds;
they conspire with the rains
to make an empty promise.

Famine looms,
but our guardians say gems go for peanuts,
there is not enough to share.
Famished, we idle as moons pass.
We will wait for a crescent one, a better promise.
I do not know for how long;
Only minions wait in silence...

living in the moment (October 2017)
Victor Gordon Musara

The land lay desolate,
marred by its caretaker
who rent it for a fortune

The land lies desolate
gutted by the undertaker
to bury the one who lived in the moment
but forgot the adage:
The land was borrowed from our
children's children's children...

Muchena Mountain by Godfrey Sagotora
Photography

Muchena is our source of pride, it is the source of ancestral powers and connection we have when it comes to rainmaking. When the mountain sends us signals of forthcoming rains we will prepare our lands and surely the rains will fall

Title: The Gravel Maker
Photography

"…And to decide on themes implies the imposition of a fiction, a 'necessary illusion' that enables our finite perceptions to gain purchase on potentiality… I am not afraid of the sounds of the streets, the collision of sound as the afternoon began its fading, neighbours growing annoyed, the various languages, the irrational pangs and songs of The Gravel Marker working hard besides the road…" (Extracted from *Peace of the Senses: How to Fight the FAGS)*

Title: Registers of Loss
Experimental Photography

Sometime in the mid-1990s this pool was our favourite place to swim, to bask in the sands around it, or on top of the rock you see disappearing to the left of the photo. With the boys of our village we would hang there, especially in the dry winter season when they were a lot less tasks to do at home. This place was our entertainment centre, where we would spend the whole day, sometimes talking boys' stuff, about girls mostly. Thereabouts 1996 a tragedy struck! Two kids of the Terera family drowned in that pool, and were found later near those sands encroaching on the pool. It was a fairly deep pool but anyone who knew how to swim would swim their way out of it. The kids knew how to swim, but they drowned and it was difficult to comprehend why they drowned at first. But from the day they died and for the next two weeks that pool had a dense cover of frothing suds of water on its top. It was the only pool in the whole of the Nyajezi River with these frothing suds, and it became scary visiting it. We watched the froth from a bit far. By then everyone knew it was the mermaids that had taken these kids. This pool was not suspected to have these mermaids... for there is another pool a bit down the river which was known to have mermaids, and the Medicine Woman of our village would deep into it for days to find strengthening from these mermaids. Her call was that she had received from the mermaid. All of a sudden we disbanded playing around it, and for years it was a monster around us. Whilst in western myth mermaids are taken to be strange beautiful creatures, in my world they are dangerous in that when they take you to their bodings in the water, there is danger it would be your last breaths. In our tradition if your relatives so much as weep a single tear whilst you are in these mythical creatures' bodings then these creatures would definitely kill you and abandon you. But if your relatives do not shed tears at your disappearance, then you are initiated into these mythical creatures' world, and when you leave the pool, after several months of initiation, also after your family had brewed beer and done a ceremony to call you back to life, then you will return a super healer. There is no powerful medicine woman than that of the mermaid's calling. We were scared of the possibility of this happening to us. Maybe what inspired me to take the photo of it is because of how pathetic it now looks as it dries in the winter dry season, as the devastation to the river takes its toll on its pool. Maybe I am saying to it that it doesn't' scare me anymore. But as you can see in the photo I added a background of a found painting, and those colourful bubbles you see depicts the froth suds that this pool had. I am trying to landscape, reimagining, reimaging what it was like in those two weeks, and in another instance I am playing truant on the pool, or the said to be mermaids that took the Terera kids. Maybe I am exorcising out the pain we had to contain, in dealing with this loss so many years ago. I am also deeply pained about how we have destroyed this river. This is evidence of it. It used to be a beautiful river, deep white sands on its banks, lots of fishes, and now it is a pale shadow of what it was. So, as I have noted, this photo also works as those important registers of loss that humanity goes through and deal with.

Near Ngundu Halt by Nicky Roselli
Oil on Canvas

In this painting I wanted to show the almost casual grandeur of the landscape in the area south of Masvingo where I used to live. I was interested in the combination of monumental rock formations combined with the signs of day to day movement of the residents of the area: the road, the paths and the bicycle.

133

The Climb by Nicky Roselli
Oil on Canvas

'The Climb' was inspired by a trip I did with my brother and sister to Mount Nyangani in the Eastern Highlands. The Nyanga area is a place that is very dear to our hearts and holds a lot of collective family memory. It was also a visual metaphor for life and the uphill climb that Zimbabweans were facing at the time and unfortunately still are.

The Rain God (Mt.Muozi) by Sally Scott
Chalk pastel

This magnificent mountain was a central feature of my childhood. It was the ever present guardian, that watched over us as we lived our idyllic days on a cattle ranch in Nyanga. It was a mystical mountain, and we treated it with great respect. This is my tribute to my memory of it.

Chimanimani Aloe by Sally Scott
Chalk pastel

This painting was done after a trip to the Chimanimani Mountains in Eastern Zimbabwe. I was captivated by the magnificent rock formations and this splendid aloe that had found root in the crack in a rock. Like the Zimbabwean people, it is able to survive on the bare minimum and has become for me another positive symbol of survival.

Nyangui Aloes by Sally Scott
Chalk pastel

As a child, I spent many days exploring the ancient ruins that cover the hillsides of Nyanga. On a return trip, I took my two young sons to visit some ruins on our old farm *Nyangui*. At the time, the countryside was very dry, having experienced 10 years of drought and a fire had recently swept through the area. As we clambered up the steep hillside, I came upon these two aloes, both parched and burnt, but still very much alive. The lesson that I took away from this encounter is that when one is well rooted, one can survive anything.

Road to Mana by Anthony Stidolph
Oil

Every now and again in my life I have come across a place which for some mysterious reason exerts this deep, personal attraction and where my need for it seems to come from the depth of my unconscious mind. The Nyanga farm, where I grew up, is one such place, so, too, is the Zambezi Valley to which I have made numerous trips. Both are places which helped shape who I am, they are slices of my past, and by revisiting them in these two paintings I felt I was not only attempting to rediscover who I am but was also looking for clues as to my own future. As such, I look upon them as precious keepsakes of the past, visual memories of two places I have lived in and loved.

Sedze, Nyanga by Anthony Stidolph
Oil

Birchenough Bridge by Kudakwashe Nhevera

The bridge is a nostalgic structure of my childhood reminding of the 20c coin that used to make up most of my memories. In essence, after being away from home for so long these are the memories of home I hold onto.

Vakomana Vemvura by Kudakwashe Nhevera

Capturing the lifestyle of a rural life in typical Zimbabwe, with trips to the borehole for the household's water. It tells of a simpler lifestyle away from the hustle of a busy city life.

The Artfarm by Kudakwashe Nhevera

Winner of The Art Farm Competition, 2014. This painting is an artist interpretation of the theme Art Farm. It's a combination of contemporary ideas put together on palette to express, in a modest way, what can be an art farm.